Routledge Revivals

Industrial Relations in the Future

First published in 1984, *Industrial Relations in the Future* highlights probable developments in Britain's system of industrial relations into the 1990s. It also provides a basis for further and detailed analysis and debate of issues central to the nation's future. Written by distinguished scholars in their respective fields, the three main sections give reviews from three contrasting traditions-mainstream industrial relations, industrial sociology and management, and labour economics. These accounts are highly complementary in the ways in which, in each and every case, issues of collective bargaining, managerial strategy and union response, and the behaviour of governments are all set against a broad backcloth of economic, political, and social changes. The authors see the ultimate outcome as depending greatly on the policies and types of action of organised labour, managements and governments, and possibly of wider social movements as well. This book will be an essential read for scholars and researchers of labour economics, industrial sociology, economics, and public policy.

Industrial Relations in the Future

Trends and Possibilities in Britain over the Next Decade

Michael Poole, William Brown, Jill Rubery, Keith Sisson, Roger Tarling, and Frank Wilkinson

First published in 1984
by Routledge & Kegan Paul Ltd.

This edition first published in 2022 by Routledge
2 Park Square, Milton Park, Abingdon, Oxon, OX14 4RN

and by Routledge
605 Third Avenue, New York, NY 10017

Routledge is an imprint of the Taylor & Francis Group, an informa business

Publisher's Note
The publisher has gone to great lengths to ensure the quality of this reprint but points out that some imperfections in the original copies may be apparent.

Disclaimer
The publisher has made every effort to trace copyright holders and welcomes correspondence from those they have been unable to contact.

A Library of Congress record exists under ISBN: 0710201451

ISBN: 978-1-032-20109-2 (hbk)
ISBN: 978-1-003-26230-5 (ebk)
ISBN: 978-1-032-20119-1 (pbk)

Book DOI 10.4324/9781003262305

Industrial relations in the future

Trends and possibilities in Britain over the next decade

Michael Poole, William Brown, Jill Rubery, Keith Sisson,
Roger Tarling and Frank Wilkinson

Routledge & Kegan Paul
London, Boston, Melbourne and Henley

First published in 1984
by Routledge & Kegan Paul plc

14 Leicester Square, London WC2H 7PH, England

9 Park Street, Boston, Mass. 02108, USA

464 St Kilda Road, Melbourne,
Victoria 3004, Australia and

Broadway House, Newtown Road,
Henley-on-Thames, Oxon RG9 1EN, England

Printed in Great Britain
by Billing & Sons Ltd, Worcester

Library of Congress Cataloging in Publication Data

Main entry under title:
Industrial relations in the future.

Bibliography; p.
Includes index.
1. Industrial relations--Great Britain. I. Poole,
Michael. II. Title.
HD8391.I477 1984 331'.0941 84-4858

British Library CIP available

ISBN 0-7102-0145-1

Contents

Tables and figures

TABLES

FIGURE

Preface

The origins of this book may be traced to an initiative by the Department of Employment to commission three major reviews of likely developments in Britain's system of industrial relations over the next decade. This unique venture seemed to us to demand a wider audience and, without any major modifications, the three contributions are printed here to enable our thinking to be communicated to the wider academic community and to the general public. Following the introduction, the reviews are set out in alphabetical order since, given that there was no overwhelming intellectual case for choosing a different sequence of presentation, this seemed to us to be the fairest way to proceed.

This prefatory note also enables the authors to convey appreciation to those whose efforts were valuable in ensuring that this work came to fruition. Considerable credit is due to Peter Brannen and Neil Millward of the Department of Employment for proposing the original venture, although they clearly bear no responsibility whatsoever for the views expressed by each contributor. Peter Hopkins and David Stonestreet of Routledge & Kegan Paul also deserve to be mentioned for their encouragement and support of this unique project. The 'Industrial Relations Journal' of Nottingham printed a shortened version of the contribution by William Brown and Keith Sisson entitled Industrial relations in the next decade (vol. 14, no. 1, spring 1983) and are thanked for raising no objections to our publishing the longer piece here. William Brown and Keith Sisson are grateful for the assistance and ideas of a large number of colleagues in the Industrial Relations Research Unit and the School of Industrial and Business Studies at the University of Warwick, and in particular Paul Edwards and Philip Way. More specific attribution is prevented by the need to absolve them from final responsibility for all opinions and judgments expressed. Michael Poole would particularly like to thank Kath Hollister for typing a substantial part of this work with unfailing courteousness and good humour and Jane Sparks of the University of Wales Institute of Science and Technology Aberconway Library for her valuable assistance in tracing some difficult references for the bibliography.

Introduction

The future of any national system of industrial relations is always an issue which occasions considerable academic and popular interest. In Britain this concern is of course particularly marked on account of the concentration in the media and by the general public on problems of union-management relationships and because the comparative maturity of industiral relations scholarship has made this a particularly fruitful area for analysis.

Naturally there can be no certainty about the exact shape and character of union-management relations in the decade ahead. Indeed, even the more specific patterns of collective bargaining and their links with broader, economic, political and social movements are by no means easy to forecast. But to highlight probable developments in industrial relations is valuable for at least three main reasons; first, it enables various theoretical propositions and general trends to be examined and elicited as a basis for prediction; second, it is particularly relevant to the central economic and industrial policies of the main political parties; and third, it stimulates the intellectual imagination to search for fresh, even visionary, initiatives and strategies for the reform of institutions and relationships.

In each of the main sections of this book a wealth of ideas and research data are marshalled to shed light on the main ways in which Britain's industrial relations system is likely to develop in the forthcoming decade. The contributions represent rather different academic traditions (mainstream industrial relations, industrial sociology and management, and labour economics) with the upshot that, in the following pages, three highly complementary but contrasting accounts are presented. There are thus several major points of agreement in each survey (for example, on the effects of unemployment and on the importance of relating industrial relations phenomena to broader economic, political and social movements); but certain divergent points of emphasis on the likely patterns of stability and change in the years ahead are also apparent.

In Part 1, Brown and Sisson, drawing upon the resources of the School of Industrial and Business Studies and the Economic and Social Research Council Industrial Relations Research Unit at

Warwick University, begin by emphasising the considerable problems and pitfalls of making sensible predictions. As they point out, a forecast made in the early 1960s would have been unlikely to identify the two critical developments of that decade: the rise of the shop steward system and the massive increase in government intervention in collective bargaining. Similarly, projections in the early 1970s would have neglected the considerable industrial relations consequences of a five-fold increase in unemployment and double figure inflation. Hence, while from the vantage point of the early to mid-1980s the role of management is almost certain to be a dominant characteristic of the evolving system of industrial relations, this outcome is by no means inevitable.

Moreover, as Brown and Sisson point out, the political context of industrial relations has increased substantially in importance accompanying the steady growth in government intervention over the past twenty years. However, there has been a tendency for legislation to favour either the interests of employers or trade unions and hence to be subject to marked changes when particular governments repeal their predecessors' labour laws and institutions. Nevertheless, the questions of the immunities of trade unions from civil actions in industrial disputes and union security (in particular, the legal regulations of the closed shop and related practices) are likely to be central to current and future labour legislation.

Turning to the economic context of industrial relations, high levels of unemployment are viewed as the most important single influence on union-management relations in the next decade. Indeed, it is salutary to note that the considerable demand for labour was one of the most critical influences underlying the development of post-war industrial relations in Great Britain. However, the prospects of job loss could either make employees and organised labour more defensive and restrictive in their working practices or, on the contrary, more adaptable and flexible.

In recent years it has become clear that the patterns of industrial relations in the private and public sectors are very different. In the private sector there have been major changes in the size, ownership and control and internal organisation of companies that have substantially affected industrial relations. These have been reflected in three main developments which are likely to feature prominently in Britain's pattern of industrial relations in the next decade. First and foremost, there has been an upsurge of single-employer bargaining which is largely explicable in terms of a series of steps by individual employers to regain control over the conduct of work. Second, there has been the development of more identifiable managerial styles in industrial relations.

Here the movement from constitutional to consultative modes may be checked by the low level of economic activity and either sophisticated paternalism or more directive approaches (which lack a coherent style) may become increasingly common. Third, there has been a decline in the traditional role of employers' associations. Although the prospects for employers' associations (especially the Confederation of British Industry) in the new climate of the 1980s are intriguing, the exceptional opportunities for revival in the recession are unlikely to be seized.

In the public sector, the principal pressures on union-management relations stem from commercial markets and from governments anxious to control public expenditure. In the 1970s there was a dramatic change in the approach to industrial relations with managerial and negotiational rather than administrative practices becoming ascendant. Moreover, in the public sector, incomes policies are inevitably of considerable importance. Indeed, as Brown and Sisson observe, there is a very strong case for a comprehensive approach to pay here even if, in practice, it is only likely to emerge after a series of expensive disputes. But to remove up to 5 million employees from 'the annual agony of pay settlement' by an imaginative policy on pay backed up by comparability machinery would undoubtedly be an attractive proposition for the reform of Britain's industrial relations.

Turning to the trade unions, Brown and Sisson note that in recent years there has been a fall in union membership following the peak of union density of 55 per cent in 1979. Moreover, even though the pattern of overall density is not easy to forecast, since it could alter rapidly depending upon wider political changes, a decline in the number of unions is anticipated in the next decade. The central problems in union organisation include the attempts to forge solidarity across a bargaining unit and to match the level of bargaining to the level of management control. Moreover, in the next decade there is likely to be a demand for internal cohesion and discipline within trade unions at the expense of rank-and-file action.

The issues of conflict and control are also seen by Brown and Sisson to be of considerable significance for Britain's industrial relations system in the decade ahead. There may well be a slow decline in the underlying trend in the number of strikes, partly because of reforms in collective bargaining machinery, but also on account of the shift away from manufacturing to services. However, the total number of working days lost through industrial disputes in a given year is significantly affected by the number of very large stoppages which are not so easy to predict.

The question of the control of enterprises may well centre on the extent to which employers emphasise a 'new realism' and exploit their market power in a recession or alternatively develop their controls and procedures in an imaginative way. But, as Brown and Sisson conclude, if the first option is typically endorsed and the opportunities for better co-ordinated bargaining structures are missed, the likelihood is that the end of the recession will leave the system of industrial relations no more advanced than it was in the 1970s.

In the second part of this volume, there is an attempt by Poole to establish an overall framework of analysis in order to facilitate meaningful prediction. The wider environmental aspects in such an analysis include structural conditions (the state, economic forces, technology, power and structured social inequality) and subjective elements (culture, values and ideas). The internal factors which bear upon labour-management relationships encompass the institutional structure of industrial relations (including collective bargaining structure, the formation of the trade unions and the social composition and structure of management and employers' associations), organisational contingencies (structural and attitudinal), and power and power conflicts in actual bargaining encounters.

In the first section of the review, the broad environmental changes are examined. The increasing role of the state is analysed against a possible overall trend towards 'corporatism' and, more specifically, towards the increasing role of the legislature in industrial relations. Economic conditions are also recognised as likely to have a considerable impact on Britain's system of industrial relations in the next decade. The main strategic shift in economic resources is seen to be in the direction of activities in a 'post-industrial' society, but employment concentration, inflation and unemployment will be of fundamental significance for the pattern which ultimately emerges. However, changes in the 'ideology of work' and a reduction in the division between home and work and paid and unpaid wage labour may also be influential.

It would be difficult to overestimate the consequences for industrial relations of changes in technology in the period in question. This applies particularly to the micro-electronic revolution, but the broad movement towards automated modes of manufacturing (highlighted by the so-called 'technical implications' school) is also fundamental. The implications of such changes for social integration, however, could clearly depend upon the values of main parties to industrial relations. The overall distribution of power in the wider society and in the patterns of structured social inequality are also vital issues. It is almost certain, however, that the relevant trends of the post-war period (full employment, welfare measures, changing social attitudes, the 'democratic current' and technical innovations) are unlikely to be particularly beneficial to trade unions and the workforce in the next ten years.

Considerable emphasis is also placed by Poole on the significance of choice in shaping the framework of industrial relations which ultimately emerges, even though a further decline in the 'tradition of voluntarism' is seen as a likely prospect. But the rather different attitudes of the principal parties (the government commitment to the problem of order, the focus of the labour movement on egalitarian-democratic values and managers on a variety of professional, 'human-resourcing' and human relations strategies in the search for profit and efficiency and enterprise control) imply that there are highly complex potential outcomes.

The second section of Poole's report involves a detailed examination of the main industrial relations groups (employers' associations and management, the trade unions and the legislature). In the case of employers' associations, a continued (and even enhanced) role for these organisations as advisory bodies is foreseen but there is unlikely to be a return to their earlier significance for collective bargaining agreements in national negotiations. Considerable importance, however, is attached to managerial strategies in industrial relations in the 1980s and early 1990s. More specifically, the trend towards an increasingly professional and specialised managerial group is predicted to continue; industrial relations policies are also liable to become increasingly sophisticated in design, comprehensive and formal in scope and informed by the input of knowledge from a variety of 'behavioural science' disciplines; an extended international dimension to industrial relations initiatives is expected and 'human resourcing' strategies will probably be further in evidence in the next ten years. However, it is argued that managerial policy in labour relations may focus more on individual employees and less on shop stewards and other plant-based organisations of labour than was the case in the 1970s.

Changes in the trade unions also constitute an interesting theme in the overall analysis. Recruitment will tend to take place in a relatively hostile environment for the trade unions. Overall density is less likely to expand at the rate experienced between 1968 and 1980, while substantial technical and economic changes will be a spur to substantial merger activity and to a concentration of membership in the largest associations. The pattern of occupational change will also facilitate a further growth of white-collar, professional and managerial trade unions at the expense of manual working sections. Shop stewards may retain their importance within trade unions but workplace-based unionism is vulnerable to the exigencies of the economic climate of the 1980s (and especially to high levels of unemployment). Meanwhile, in respect of union government, factionalism could continue to be a major issue in internal trade union organisation and, on present trends, a considerable measure of industrial conflict and trade union militancy outside the highly competitive sectors remains highly probable.

With regard to legislation on industrial relations, this is likely to feature prominently in Britain over the next decade, though its precise form will reflect prevailing political conditions. It is conceivable, however, that European legislation will affect labour issues in Britain in the forthcoming years and, above all, will encompass such measures as security and conditions of employment.

In the third section of Poole's analysis, areas where key developments (with substantial implications for policy) are predicted are examined in more depth and detail. These include: industrial democracy and employee participation, worksharing, quality of working life programmes, European initiatives, trade union legislation, managerial 'human resourcing' strategies, the position of women and minority ethnic groups in the employment relationship, incomes policy and industrial conflict. Finally, the signal weakness of the British industrial relations system is traced to an excessive reliance on collective bargaining since this is seen to ensure that power is ultimately decisive in the rewards which accrue to various groups in the working population with the result that issues of control rather than creativity assume particular significance in the employment relationship.

In the final report, Rubery, Tarling and Wilkinson examine industrial relations issues in the next decade on the basis of a number of macroeconomic assumptions. The overall contribution is concerned with how economic and social conditions could put pressure on custom and practice in the workplace together with the way in which the collective bargaining framework and the trade union movement responds, and the degree and nature of political support given to legislation.

There is a whole range of macroeconomic forecasts for the 1980s, some considerably more optimistic than others. There is fairly common agreement, however, that the number of jobs available will fall short of the number required to satisfy those people in the population who wish to work and that, for the population as a whole, real income per capita will need to grow quite slowly for much of the period. These broad macroeconomic developments provide the context in which industrial relations in the 1980s must develop and, from a starting point of high unemployment and constrained real incomes, mean that the incidence of unemployment and low income is likely to increase. The major features of these developments are discussed by Rubery, Tarling and Wilkinson with attention being given to the assumptions made about individual and collective behaviour within the major economic strategies currently advocated by politicians and economists.

This discussion of the macroeconomic context and its implications for management and labour is important first because it indicates the changes that management or labour may seek in their bargaining position, and second because it helps identify the areas where groups within government, management and labour might find themselves in agreement as well as in conflict. However, even though areas for agreement will be found - for example government, management and some parts of organised labour may accept that higher unemployment is a necessary counterpart to restoring competitiveness - such policies will nevertheless give rise to conflict between capital and labour and the factors that will determine which groups will bear the burden of adjustment to changed macroeconomic conditions. The increased concern by capital to maintain and increase flexibility of labour costs coincides with a time when trade unions become increasingly concerned with job security and job protection. However the question of who bears the burden of adjustment, capital or labour, cannot be answered simply, because of the heterogeneity of firms and the heterogeneity of labour. A move towards lower-paid, more flexible labour provides an alternative to capital attempting to break down existing collective agreements; but the end result might be similar as the restructuring towards secondary employment undermines the basis for protection in primary employment. But to provide a proper analysis of the impact on industrial relations it is necessary to assess the strategies to be employed by management and labour to meet these conditions.

In section 4 of Rubery, Tarling and Wilkinson's report, management's interest in achieving flexible unit labour costs in relation to output is shown to be increasing and likely to be pursued at national, industry and enterprise levels as well as in the workplace while labour is shown to be faced with an increasing attack on living standards, defined to include not only real earnings but also access to employment, vulnerability in employment and more generally the 'social wage'. In this section, however, it is noted that product market, technical and social factors may lead to a divided response by either management or labour. It is therefore also relevant to consider what is the balance of power and who is vulnerable when issues are dealt with at the different levels of national, industry and plant bargaining. However labour's response to these attacks is not purely individual or sectional in nature but has its roots in the system of social reproduction, and the location of labour's organisation and collective action within the social and family system as well as within the workplace may in the long run lead to a collective and unified response.

Section 5 of Rubery, Tarling and Wilkinson's contribution contains a more detailed discussion of specific issues. These are grouped under four separate headings. In the first, there is an examination of inflation and incomes policy which will remain central to economic policy choice in the 1980s. It is a matter of some relevance whether incomes policies are run implicitly as now through unemployment and cash limits or explicitly as a direct policy instrument. The effects on the structure of earnings between and within firms are likely to be quite different although the concentration of low pay among certain jobs would remain a feature of both. The second heading groups together special employment measures and youth employment. These are, in one sense, social responses to the consequences of economic policy which is designed to foster competitiveness. It is argued that they have some important effects on the structure of the employment but do little in the long run to alter the incidence of low pay and unemployment. Youth employment in particular is liable to be an increasing problem and is potentially very socially divisive. The third heading relates to legislative change and here attention is focused on the issue of minimum wage legislation. This is, and will remain, a major policy debate and is central to the conflict between motives of economic efficiency and demands for social justice. The fourth heading looks at the machinery for voluntary collective bargaining at local and national level and explores the possibility of support for or opposition to measures to promote industrial democracy.

The final section of Rubery, Tarling and Wilkinson's report draws together the discussion of section 5 and attempts to point out how issues faced in the 1970s, or in earlier crises, may differ in the 1980s. These issues are not new, but they may be heavily influenced by the economic and political threat to the welfare state and legislative attempts to shift the balance of power against labour. An important feature of the 1980s is undoubtedly seen to be the growing divergence between capital and labour under conditions of slow growth and the exacerbation of conflict in the workplace because of the impact on national decisions. But the threat to organised labour may, at least initially, lead the trade unions to attempt to restrict access to jobs and a unified response from the labour movement may only emerge from action taken at the social level and not initially in the workplace.

The three main parts of this book thus represent contrasting styles and traditions and diverse approaches to analysing industrial relations. They are, however, highly complementary in the ways in which, in each and every case, issues of collective bargaining, managerial strategy and union response, and the behaviour of governments, are set against a broad backcloth of economic, political and social changes. In all the reports, therefore, there is an acknowledgment of the considerable importance of these wider conditions in shaping the patterns of labour relations which ultimately develop in Britain. In no instance is a wholly determinist perspective deployed and, within certain probable limits, the ultimate outcome is seen to depend greatly on the policies and types of action of organised labour, managements and governments and possibly of wider social movements as well. It is comparatively rare for the representatives of three contrasting traditions (mainstream industrial relations, industrial sociology and management, and labour economics) to come together in a venture of this type. The outcome should be a volume which will not provide simple answers to inevitably highly complex problems but which will highlight a number of possible paths and directions for the evolution of the British system of industrial relations in the years ahead and provide a basis for further and detailed analysis and debate.

Part 1

Current trends and future possibilities

William Brown and Keith Sisson

Cautions and contexts

'Dreams and predictions', observed Francis Bacon four centuries ago, 'ought to serve but for winter talk by the fireside.' If this essay is to be of use it should start on a note of humility. Had it been written in 1962 it would have underestimated the rise of the shop steward and would have neglected totally the massive increase in government intervention in collective bargaining in the following decade. In 1972, when industrial action in the non-mining public sector was still a novelty, no forecast could have envisaged a decade in which unemployment was to increase fivefold and during which inflation was to remain in double figures. A reader in the 1990s may consider that the merits of this study lie less in its cautious attempts at extrapolation than in the doubts it casts on some of the more seductive predictions occasioned by the particular circumstances of the early to mid-1980s.

Our central purpose is not prediction. It is to stimulate thought about future developments in British industrial relations through a discussion of current trends and of the likelihood of their continuing. In the sections that follow we shall consider the pattern of change in the private sector, in the public sector, and in trade union organisation, and shall conclude with a discussion of changes in conflict and control. But, especially in Britain, the conduct of industrial relations cannot be divorced from the wider realms of politics and the economy; they all interact. It is thus necessary to start with a discussion of the range of possible political and economic contexts. This is only of value if we also discuss the extent to which it is possible to associate changes in industrial relations behaviour with changes in these contexts.

It should be stressed that there is no 'model' that can be used for prediction in the normal sense. First, there is no simple direction of causation; while bargaining behaviour may be influenced by the level of unemployment, the government's efforts at control over that level will also be influenced by its beliefs about bargaining behaviour. Second, relatively few of the variables that might be considered relevant can be expressed in numbers and, as Marshall observed, 'the application of exact mathematical methods to those which can is nearly always a waste of time, while in the large majority of cases it is positively misleading.' Third, even where, as in the case of strike incidence and trade union membership, quantitative models have been used to good explanatory effect, they would be of poor predictive value, being subject to intermittent structural shifts for reasons outside the models and having been developed for very different levels of inflation and unemployment from those to which we are now accustomed. Fourth, in industrial relations, more than in most economic behaviour, past responses to a given phenomenon are a poor guide to future responses. An activity so essentially concerned with collective decision-making and institutional development involves learning and adaptation behaviour that place it beyond the reach of normal time-series modelling methods.

Our focus is the relatively narrow one of collective relations between employers and employees. The fact that there are complementary analyses of sociological and economic aspects of future developments in the field of employment causes the scope of this essay to be somewhat narrower than if it were to stand on its own. It will, for example, barely touch upon changes in the composition of the labour force, questions of pay structure, or broader aspects of participation. The nature of the commission calls for a broad-brush approach rather than a survey of research literature and, accordingly, we have limited our citing of other work.

The political context

The importance of the political context to the conduct of collective bargaining has increased with the steady increase in government intervention over the past twenty years. It is unlikely to diminish so long as industrial unrest, especially in the public sector, remains a political issue, and so long as industrial and counter-inflationary policies remain important parts of the governmental function. Leaving for later consideration the role of the government as an employer, we consider first industrial relations legislation.

Governments have moved from generally avoiding legislative intervention in collective bargaining in the 1950s, through a largely non-partisan phase of legislation on matters such as training and redundancy in the 1960s, to substantial and controversial intervention in the 1970s and early 1980s. The tendency for legislation to be increasingly partisan towards the interests of either employers or trade unions, and the associated tendency for governments to repeal their predecessors' labour laws and institutions, demands predictive caution. But, whether or not these cycles moderate, it is difficult to see either Labour or Conservative governments (or, on the basis of recent statements, the SDP-Liberal Alliance) leaving collective bargaining alone.

Two broad areas are likely to remain on the political agenda. The first is the question of trade unions' immunities from civil actions in industrial disputes. The form of legal moves to extend or limit these (possibly in conjunction with attempts to alter the legal status of collective agreements) remains uncertain. At least as uncertain would be trade union responses and judicial interpretation. This would remain so even if the system of immunities were replaced by positive rights. The problem of the boundary between what is lawful and what is unlawful would remain the controversial issue. Second, questions of trade union security and, in particular, the legal regulation of the closed shop and related practices, are likely to remain contentious. The impact of fresh individual rights is likely to be heavily influenced by the extent to which, in any particular situation, managers and unions seek to preserve their existing collective bargaining arrangements.

What might be the consequences of an increasingly unsupportive governmental attitude towards collective bargaining? First it seems safe to say that practices will not undergo substantial change throughout the very large tracts of employment where collective bargaining is an integral part of the management process. Throughout the public sector and much of, for example, engineering and chemicals, managements can be expected to go to considerable lengths to prevent legislative innovation disrupting established bargaining arrangements. But where collective bargaining is non-existent or shallowly rooted, as in much of the tertiary sector and small, subcontracting manufacturing establishments, it can be expected to retreat. Specific items of legislation, such as those providing opportunities to challenge closed shops, would probably play a lesser part in weakening collective bargaining than the more diffuse symbolic impact of the withdrawal of explicit government support.

The second observation suggested by past experience is that legislative intervention in collective bargaining, whether designed to extend or to inhibit it, modifies its conduct in important and unintended ways. There is strong evidence that a major cause of the substantial increase in the professionalism of industrial relations management over the 1970s - the managers concerned would say the single major cause - was the increase in labour legislation over the period. This stimulated the development of single-employer bargaining (at the expense of industry-wide agreements) and often increased the centralisation of control over industrial relations matters in multi-plant companies. Future legislation that might involve financial penalties for either employers or unions, or that might jeopardise bargaining relationships, will tend to have the same effect.

Incomes policies have been among the most important forms of government intervention in collective bargaining. No government since the Second World War has left office without first feeling obliged reluctantly to embark on some form of incomes policy. Some have lost office because of the consequences. With inflation now apparently endemic in the world economy, and with Britain's decentralised bargaining system proving particularly potent in amplifying it, there is every reason to suppose that, if levels of unemployment are to be brought down, incomes policies will be a recurrent issue.

What can be said about the form they might take? We shall return to the possibilities of a long-term policy based upon greater co-ordination of collective bargaining after considering the roles of the CBI and TUC. Short-term policies have been so diverse in content over the past fifteen years that it is hard to speculate on future endeavours. Dangers of political embarrassment are reduced if penalties for non-compliance are directed at employers rather than trade unions; in this respect the current interest in tax-based incomes policies continues an approach that has previously used price controls and government contracts as sanctions. Chances of success also tend to be greater if the TUC can be persuaded at least to acquiesce. Because of this, governmental efforts to introduce incomes policies tend to be associated with a rise in the relative status of the TUC and, to a lesser extent, the CBI. But, even when the policies are successful, this does not imply a withering of the institutions of bargaining at lower levels. Recent years have seen unprecedented peace-time use of incomes policies coincide with an unprecedented consolidation of single-employer and workplace bargaining. Unless the policy takes the form of simple indexation it is likely to leave productivity and much else still to be bargained over at the workplace.

A different form of long-term incomes policy is that of statutory intervention to combat low pay. Equal pay legislation achieved some notable gains for women in the first half of the 1970s, but since 1976 these have barely been maintained. Further progress is unlikely unless the intervention is sufficiently penetrating to reduce discrimination in recruitment, promotion, training, and work organisation. On this, as on other questions of labour law, it is difficult to envisage EEC initiatives having anything other than a minor demonstrative impact for the foreseeable future.

On the problem of low pay for both sexes, the bi-partisan policy of gradually dismantling the wages council system since the 1960s has been called into question. Despite the opportunity since 1975 to establish statutory joint industrial councils with enforcement powers, collective bargaining has generally not developed as a suitable substitute to wages council regulation, inadequate though that may have been. While some influential political voices speak of further abolition as a means of generating jobs, others argue that the employment effects would be minimal and, supported by the Advisory, Conciliation and Arbitration Service, press the case for new or revived wages councils. The likely outcome of the debate is unclear.

However hot and cold governments may blow on the practice of collective bargaining they are unlikely to undermine ACAS. But, while the advisory work of this body continues to expand, and its individual conciliation services remain in consistent and high demand, the number of calls on it for collective conciliation has tended to decline in recent years. Although in part this reflects a general decline in the level of disputes, it does not lead us to expect conciliation and arbitration to play a substantially increased role in British industrial relations in the next decade.

The economic context

Even professional economic forecasters would make their excuses when asked to talk about so far as a decade ahead. To some extent we can do no more than indicate the great range of uncertainty that possible future economic circumstances present for the conduct of industrial relations. Uncertainty, for example, about the size of reserves of petroleum, and about its world price, is so great that the associated range of possible sterling exchange rates could imply anything from a major recovery of our export industries through to their faster demise. Similarly, in a world of floating exchange rates it requires a reckless degree of optimism to imagine domestic price inflation falling below 5 per cent per annum; on the other hand a memory dating back only to 1975 will suggest that unfettered bargaining could quickly take it over 25 per cent.

In one respect, however, there is substantial agreement among the forecasters. Most models predict the level of unemployment to be as high as at the moment at least until 1985. The prospect of labour-replacing technological innovation and the possibility of continuing cuts in public service employment make it unlikely that there will be a substantial decline in the number out of work in subsequent years. We thus face the prospect of a prolonged period with unemployment levels which are exceptionally high by comparison with the preceding forty years. Since a high level of demand for labour is generally accepted as having been one of the most important influences underlying the development of post-war British industrial relations, this major transformation is clearly of great importance for the present discussion. What can be said about the impact of sustained high unemployment upon industrial relations?

Little systematic research is available to inform us on the

impact of high unemployment levels upon either individual or collective behaviour. Social psychologists and sociologists have studied characteristics of the unemployed and what happens to those made redundant, but this does not tell us much about those still in work. Since, however, an important consequence of rising unemployment is that a rising proportion of those in employment have past experience of being unemployed (fewer than a third of registered unemployed have been continuously registered for more than a year), one relevant question is how that experience influences subsequent attitudes at work. Does, for example, the experience raise political consciousness or increase individualistic apathy? A recent American study suggests that the experience of unemployment has little impact upon either social ideology or political behaviour for those affected (Schlozman and Verba, 1979). Other complex and almost unresearched areas are those of employees' responses to increased risk of job loss, to reduced chances of moving to other jobs, and to reduced opportunity to fulfil their work potential. There is evidence that people in work have unrealistically optimistic beliefs about the nature of unemployment and their likelihood of gaining fresh employment; this misperception may help explain the continued and paradoxical drawing power of voluntary redundancy schemes.

Evidence on collective behaviour under high unemployment is even more scanty. A key question to which we shall return is whether and under what circumstances the increased risk of job loss makes employees more defensive and restrictive in their working practices or, on the contrary, more 'realistic' and flexible. Another is whether the slackening in demand for labour causes trade unions to seek to raise the level of bargaining and find protection in larger coalitions.

One exploratory device which we shall use is reference back to experience in the 1930s when unemployment was comparably high. At its peak, in 1932, 17 per cent of the working population (measured on a basis comparable with the present) was out of work (Feinstein, 1972). In 1982 the figure is arguably misleadingly low at the official figure of about 12 per cent because of the large number of women who have withdrawn from the unemployment register and because of the extent of special employment measures. In so far as it is possible to compare like with like over half a century, the severity of the recessions is sufficiently similar to make comparisons - with due caution - worthwhile. Certainly nothing has happened to the labour market since the war to prepare us for the upheaval to collective bargaining that may now be underway.

The private sector

Organisation

Seventy per cent of the employed labour force is in the private sector. A declining 40 per cent of these private sector employees is in manufacturing industry. It will help a consideration of developments in industrial relations to outline some of the major changes in organisation that have occurred. Some data are available only for manufacturing.

There have been substantial changes in the size of organisations. A number of aspects of industrial relations behaviour are highly sensitive to size, especially to establishment size but also the size of the wider enterprise of which it is a part (Marginson, 1982). The median size of establishment in manufacturing, having increased from 230 employees in 1930 to 480 in 1968, is now probably slowly declining. Even so, in 1978 two-fifths of employees in manufacturing worked in establishments with 1000 or more employees (Census of Production, 1978).

At least until recently the size of overall enterprise continued to grow, but at a slower pace than in the late 1950s and 1960s. Enterprises with 10,000 or more employees accounted for a quarter of manufacturing employment in 1958 but for more than a third in 1978. Over the twenty years the number of these massive enterprises increased from 74 to 83 and their average number of establishments from 30 to 40. The loss of one in five jobs in manufacturing since 1979, however, and the substantial redundancies announced by many major firms in recent years suggest that organisational size may no longer be on the increase.

The nature of ownership and control within these companies has also changed. Instead of ownership being in the hands of founding families or of a mass of private shareholders, it is increasingly a relatively small number of institutions - notably insurance companies and pension funds - that dominate. Between 1957 and 1975 the proportion of shares owned by institutional investors rose from 30 per cent to 50 per cent. It is a proportion that is likely to continue to grow and it has been authoritatively argued that this form of ownership tends to encourage further industrial concentration (Prais, 1976).

Foreign ownership has also increased. Although the rate of this is difficult to judge, in 1979, 23 per cent of the 4,000 largest private companies in Britain were owned by overseas interests (Size Report, 1979). They employed just over a million people in their British establishments. In manufacturing a little under one in five jobs are in foreign-owned firms, the great majority of these being American. Foreign owners have tended to be a catalytic force in British industrial relations, sometimes managing without collective bargaining altogether and often setting the pace in the move from multi-employer to company agreements (Brown, 1981).

Finally, there have been substantial changes in the internal organisation of these large companies. Twenty-five years ago the typical pattern was either one of highly centralised control of all functions, or one of a holding company where the separate divisions had a high degree of autonomy. Since then there has been a general move towards multi-divisional organisation in which head office maintains close control over strategic matters while allowing divisions substantial functional independence. One study of 120 large companies suggests that the proportion of them organised on multi-divisional lines rose from 42 per cent to 68 per cent between 1965 and 1971 (Steer and Cable, 1978). An important consequence of this development for collective bargaining is that, while industrial relations matters are usually dealt with at or below the level of the division, they are dependent upon strategic decisions which are made at the level of the whole company.

Bargaining structure

In 1980, according to the DE/PSI/SSRC Workplace Industrial Relations Survey, three-quarters of private sector employees had their pay determined by some sort of arrangement between employers and trade unions. But these were not the industry-wide, multi-employer arrangements that had been dominant before and just after the war. Although it is hard to be too precise about the figures (especially in small concerns managers appear to be somewhat vague about the origins of the rates they pay), multi-employer agreements covered only 20 per cent and wages council rates only 5 per cent of private sector employees. For the remaining 50 per cent the focus of collective bargaining was a single-employer agreement at company, divisional or workplace level.

The upsurge in single-employer bargaining since the 1960s is best understood not as a deliberate flight from industry-wide multi-employer agreements (membership of employers' associations has generally been maintained), but rather the consequence of a series of steps by individual employers to regain control over the conduct of work. Thus disputes procedures based upon the workplace have spread to become almost universal; there is increased use of work study; payment by results systems are less fragmented and are under tighter control; and use of job evaluation has spread to cover over half the manufacturing workforce. The efforts to regain control are reflected in a greatly increased use of specialist industrial relations managers at factory level and also increased representation of industrial relations interests at board level.

It has already been noted that there have been changes since the war in the internal organisation of private enterprises, with a shift towards multi-divisional patterns of control. The extent to which single-employer bargaining structures have been made congruent with these control structures has varied greatly. Although there has been an increase in the number of enterprises that rely on negotiations covering more than one establishment, either at the level of the division or the company itself, they remain the minority. In 1980, according to the DE/PSI/SSRC survey, two-fifths of the employers covered by single-employer arrangements had multi-plant agreements; for the majority the agreement was still establishment-based.

In the short run there is no reason to believe that this picture will change dramatically. There is no simple explanation for the variation; it is largely a question of management strategies which, in turn, are contingent on particular circumstances. Integrated production arrangements, for example, are important in explaining why the vehicle manufacturers favour corporate bargaining. Another group of companies which appears to favour corporate agreements, those in food manufacturing, has probably been anxious to avoid the development of workplace bargaining. For the majority, however, the advantages lie with decentralised bargaining at the establishment. As well as denying the trade unions a role in the determination of broad company policy, establishment bargaining makes it possible for management to argue that its 'capacity to pay' is all-important. At the same time the outcomes can be carefully co-ordinated from divisional or company headquarters so that differences in pay and conditions within the enterprise do not become too large. The recently diminished power of shop stewards has provided a fresh twist. With less to fear from comparability arguments between different establishments, there has been a tendency for managements to take greater advantage of local market and bargaining differences. Many companies with well-established multi-plant agreements have recently introduced some sort of plant productivity bonus.

Managerial styles

No less important than the structure a company adopts for its bargaining is the 'style' of its approach. By this we mean, above all else, the centrality of collective bargaining to its management of employment relations. Four very simple categories will suffice to illustrate this underresearched concept. The first, which we might call 'sophisticated paternalism', is characterised by a deliberate attempt to avoid collective bargaining and often a refusal to recognise trade unions. Instead of coping with conflict through industrial relations procedures, the company seeks to pre-empt it through personnel techniques: careful screening of recruits, in-house training, counselling, and strong assurances of security of employment. Some of the best examples in Britain are provided by American-owned firms. A second style might be termed 'constitutional'. This sees collective bargaining, and the explicit power relationship upon which it is based, as the dominating feature of industrial government. Accordingly, great attention is given to procedural rectitude and written agreements, but little attempt is made to develop other links with the workforce. Third, there is what might be called the 'consultative' approach. This accepts collective bargaining - indeed, conducts it with great professionalism - but there is no desire to codify everything in a collective agreement. On the contrary, every attempt is made to minimise the amount of joint regulation and great emphasis is placed on joint consultation, with 'problems' having to be solved rather than 'disputes' settled.

The great majority of employers, especially those in engineering, fall into the fourth category. These might be described as the 'pragmatists' or 'opportunists'. In contrast to the first three, whose styles all embody coherent approaches to the problem of controlling and motivating employees, this group is characterised by an essentially ad hoc approach. In their case the rise of the specialist industrial relations function during the 1960s is to be seen largely as a reflection of the overburdening of line managers with industrial relations problems and the need for specialist 'fire-fighters' to help cope. It rarely reflected a commitment on the part of top management to the need to integrate industrial relations considerations to wider business and corporate plans. Recent apparently dramatic changes in practice in some 'pragmatist' companies, particularly in the treatment of shop stewards, should not be interpreted in terms of a new breed of 'macho' managers breaking fresh ground. They are more to be seen as a desperate reaction to an appalling product market situation. Their industrial relations specialists, if they have not themselves been made redundant, must shudder to think what is going to happen if ever there is an upturn.

What of the future? Although the non-union approach of 'sophisticated paternalism' may appeal to some employers, it requires considerable management resources and a growing, or at least secure, demand for the product to be successful.

Consequently, while it may become prevalent in the new high technology industries, it is difficult to envisage a significant number of established employers taking advantage of the opportunity offered by heavy unemployment and closed shop ballots to launch the sort of anti-union campaigns that have become so common in North America. Similarly, there is unlikely to be a significant increase in the number of 'constitutional' managements. Most British employers seem as wedded to informality as the trade unions; they firmly rejected Donovan's advice to extend the scope of joint regulation and did not take advantage of the opportunity provided by the Industrial Relations Act of 1971 to make collective agreements legally enforceable. In the current economic climate, with managements being able to force through changes in informal work practices with little or no opposition, formal agreements would appear to make even less sense.

The most likely move is in the direction of the 'consultative' approach. At first sight the collapse in the level of economic activity hardly appears propitious. There would also have to be considerable changes in management organisation and in the style of individual managers. Yet even some of the most aggressive managements have begun to argue that simple compliance by employees is not going to be enough if they are to match the international competition which is likely to become even more intense as the 1980s wear on. What is needed, it is argued, is far greater employee commitment which is only going to come about if the individual employee is accorded respect, and if employees, both individually and collectively, are involved in the key decisions which affect them. All this suggests that in the future there will be much more emphasis on individual personnel policies and a considerable increase in the use of quality circles, briefing groups, business and company councils and the like. This could well be linked, in a more Japanese manner, with the subcontracting of all but the essential activities of the business, with the consequence of greater security of employment for a much smaller core of permanent employees.

Employers' organisations

It might have been thought that the recession offered an exceptional opportunity for a revival of employers' organisations as bargaining agents. Spared the need to outbid each other for scarce labour, employers might be expected to unite to persuade a tattered trade union movement of the virtues of genuine multi-employer industry-wide agreements. In so doing, they could take collective bargaining over pay and other conditions outside the workplace, much as is the practice elsewhere in Western Europe (Sisson, 1984), and thereby beyond the reach of the shop stewards at whose hands managerial prerogatives have received such a battering in the post-war period. Will they seize the chance?

All the signs are that they will not. It was not, in the first place, their response to the inter-war Depression, when both the membership of the largest employers' organisation, the Engineering Employers' Federation, and the number of Joint Industrial Councils fell steadily and substantially. Nor are there signs that it is their response now. In 1979 the EEF suffered substantial defections in the face of one- and two-day stoppages over the 39-hour week. However one judges the outcome, it resulted in a weaker national agreement and has been followed by the defederation of the two largest members. In 1980 the British Printing Industries Federation had to concede the 37½-hour week when an increasing number of its member firms settled under pressure from the National Graphical Association. If we look at the large food manufacturing industry, where there is little tradition of union militancy, the picture of disunity is similar. The Food Manufacturing JIC, the Bacon Curing JIC, the Slaughtering Industry JIC, and the Cocoa, Chocolate and Confectionery JIC all failed to agree in 1980, and in 1981 all failed to agree except Food Manufacturing which eventually settled under ACAS intervention. Even in construction, where a high level of competition, high labour costs, and small workforces would appear to be strongly supportive of multi-employer bargaining, the employers have been showing signs of disunity.

Despite this, the virtual abandonment of multi-employer bargaining in Britain does not necessarily mean that employers' organisations will vanish from the scene. The great majority are also trade organisations and so represent their members' interests across a broad range of commercial issues. Evidence from the Warwick Survey suggests that the operation of an industry-wide disputes procedure is a function which continues to be valued by managements even in many of the larger enterprises (Brown, 1981). This is also true of the advisory and consultancy services which most employers' organisations have developed in recent years. Indeed, paradoxical as it may seem, some employers' organisations probably exert more influence on workplace industrial relations through the performance of these functions than they did through the negotiation of multi-employer agreements.

It could be that the CBI will come to play a more and more important role within the framework of employers' organisations. Some larger enterprises with interests in several industries are already suggesting the need for a restructuring of employers' organisations based on the CBI and a multi-industry regional network. A change in government could bring a reversal of the 1982 CBI Conference decision to reject the proposal for a national economic forum which had been supported in previous years. Similarly, other proposals contained in the CBI's discussion documents 'The Future of Pay Bargaining' (1977) and 'Pay: The Choice Ahead' (1979), including the synchronisation of pay settlements and a strike fund, could re-emerge if there was a revival in the bargaining power of trade unions and, in particular, in the ability of shop steward organisations to make coercive comparisons between employers. If such proposals were actually implemented, the CBI would begin to enjoy some of the authority of its continental counterparts which are intimately involved in collective bargaining either as bargaining agents in their own right or as the co-ordinators of settlements reached at lower levels.

The public sector

The public sector's workforce of 7 million is currently made up of approximately 2 million employees in public corporations, 1½ million in health services, 1½ million in education, 1½ million in central and local government administration, and the final half million in the police and armed forces. Over the past twenty years, despite the contraction of public corporations, employment in the public sector grew by a quarter, a growth that has been halted abruptly in the past two years. The conduct of industrial relations in the very varied industries that make up the sector has been strongly influenced by the timing and weight of pressures for greater efficiency. These have come to varying degrees both from commercial markets and from governments anxious to control public expenditure.

The range of pressures is particularly evident in the public corporations. For ease of exposition we can divide them into four groups, each, as it happens, covering roughly half a million employees: manufacturing, energy, transport, and communications. The whole manufacturing group (BSC, BS, BAe, BL and RR) are recently nationalised and have strong traditions of workplace bargaining. Under severe competitive pressure from overseas, their response has in many respects been the same as if they had stayed in the private sector. They have increased centralised controls over bargaining, in some cases in addition introducing a corporate agreement. Incentive pay schemes have been controlled, bargaining units simplified, and, alongside substantial redundancies, there have been some dramatic changes in working practices.

The energy industries - coal, electricity and gas - underwent their greatest upheaval in the 1960s, hard-pressed by the competitive pressure of cheap petroleum. In a series of productivity deals they first changed working practices and grading systems and then used payment by results to raise effort levels. The rise in the relative price of petroleum in the early 1970s placed them in a far stronger position and they are likely to remain pacesetters in public sector pay for the foreseeable future. Benefiting from reorganisation and the absence of competition, the water industry sought to join them; whether this stance will be shaken by its recent further reorganisation remains to be seen.

Competitive pressures have been and will continue to be more severe in the transport corporations (British Rail, British Airways, National Bus Company and London Transport Executive), largely because of the direct threat of alternative transport. Rising fuel costs and growing political opposition to subsidised transport increase the pressures on these relatively labour intensive industries to accept tighter working practices. By comparison the communications group (Post Office, British Telecom and the British Broadcasting Corporation) are in the relatively favoured position of having less direct threat to their existence, although the recent demand that they apply commercial criteria, threats of denationalisation, and increased governmental pressure to reduce costs create peculiar strains in organisations with deep civil service traditions.

Elsewhere in the public sector this tension between providing a service and saving cost has become, and is likely to remain, dominant. It should be emphasised how fundamentally industrial relations in these public services has changed. Even as recently as fifteen years ago national negotiations were considered sufficiently detailed to allow the manager's job at the place of work to be one of administration rather than negotiation. It would have been hard to disentangle notions of managerial prerogatives from the imperatives of the service being provided. Around the end of the 1960s, however, a combination of circumstances altered this. There was growing doubt about the efficiency of management. The Prices and Incomes Board argued that poor labour utilisation was a major cause of the relatively low pay of the public services and it urged the use of payment by results to put both right. Other enquiries, such as those of Bains in local government and Fulton in the civil service, urged more professional management. It was the deterioration in relative pay that came in 1969 with the international inflation that precipitated the first widespread industrial action. But with incentive schemes increasingly generating local bargaining problems, and wholesale reorganisations, particularly in the health service and local authorities, disrupting all manner of working and bargaining relationships, a fundamental change in the climate of industrial relations was inevitable.

Current trends and future possibilities

Although the approach to industrial relations became managerial and negotiatory rather than administrative during the early 1970s, it was still the case that the level of services was in general terms determined by demand. In the late 1970s, this changed. Underlying the very varied practices and assumptions of 'cash limits' policies is the view that the service in question is not inviolate and may have to be reduced if costs exceed some target. In accord with this, and suggesting it to be more than a passing phase, there has been a widespread re-ordering of management controls in the public services. In many instances the finance function has come to play a more visible role in industrial relations matters, with plans being vetted for their cost implications to an unprecedented extent and with tighter regulation of the pay budget. More generally there has been increased co-ordination of industrial relations decision-making. In the National Health Service, for example, monthly meetings of management side Whitley Council leaders have been introduced, along with more uniform costing techniques and efforts to co-ordinate strategy across bargaining units. In local government both the Local Authorities' Conditions of Service Advisory Board and the Association of County Councils have increased their monitoring and advisory activities with the intention of improving the consistency and timing of employer initiatives. It is hard to envisage political and economic circumstances arising in the next decade that could permit a return to the practices of the 1960s and 1970s. Industrial relations in the public services are likely to remain more tightly, and more centrally, controlled than before.

Public sector pay

However much public sector management succeeds in gaining greater control over the conduct of work, a central problem will remain the appropriate level of pay. This has not always been a problem. For the first twenty years after the war public sector pay was maintained in a fairly steady relationship with comparable pay elsewhere, keeping slightly below and moving slightly later than that in the private sector. But in the late 1960s, partly as a result of incomes policies, the gap widened. The upheaval that came in the early 1970s, forcing the public sector well ahead of the private sector by 1975, had many causes besides the unrest caused by this relative deterioration. Incentive schemes had been introduced in local authorities and public utilities, and the reorganisation of local authorities, health and water services made the newfound militancy of the workforce extremely rewarding. Equal pay legislation and threshold payments brought further gains that favoured the public sector. As had been the case ten years earlier, after 1975 it was a Labour incomes policy that worsened this relative position. By 1979 the public and private sectors were back in broad parity, but widespread discontent in the former had forced the creation of the Comparability Commission and, by 1981, the consequent settlements had again brought public sector pay ahead. It is far from clear whether the public expenditure cuts of the 1980s will reassert the traditional dominance of the private sector.

There is little prospect that, under existing arrangements, the public sector will revert to being a passive part of the national pay determination mechanism. The recent disturbance to differentials and attitudes has been too great. Public sector pay policy will be a perennial and central issue, not only because of efforts to limit labour costs and industrial disruption, but also because of the implications for national incomes policies which, in both 1974 and 1979, collapsed through pressure from this source.

There are four types of incomes policy currently being pursued in the public sector. For the armed forces, the police, and, somewhat hesitantly, the fire services, pay is indexed to national average earnings. For doctors, dentists, judges, politicians and others covered by review bodies, and also, until recently, for the civil service, pay is fixed (with varying degrees of rigour and rather irregular timing) on the basis of comparability with the private sector. For the public services of health, education and local government, there is a 'cash limit' policy; in practice the way in which this is applied in different services varies considerably in terms of assumptions, flexibility and prior negotiation. Finally, those industries which are exposed to market forces are expected to pursue a restrained form of collective bargaining. Since, however, many of these industries are dependent upon subsidies from the Exchequer or upon government permission for price rises, the outcome for them is much the same as if they had cash limits.

The varied nature of public sector employment probably makes it unavoidable that those industries exposed to product market forces should operate a circumscribed form of collective bargaining. But it is avoidable that pay policy for the public services should be so fragmented and fitful. As the Comparability Commission observed, from as far back as the nineteenth century governments have tended to fall back on comparisons with employees elsewhere when fixing the pay of their own workforce. Pressure for comparability has come in waves,

each stronger than the last, each arrested by a government incomes policy until that policy has in turn been overwhelmed by another wave which has extended the scope of comparability more widely than before. At first, each incomes

> policy has been strongly opposed to comparability; but each has subsequently begun to acknowledge that pay comparisons have a place in public sector pay settlement. (Standing Commission of Pay Comparability, 1980)

A major difficulty with the fragmented nature of past comparability exercises - whether review bodies, ad hoc enquiries, or pay research - is that they tend to be somewhat partisan, persuaded of the peculiar qualities of the occupation with which they have been preoccupied, and thus more generous in their awards (and consequently more provocative to others) than if they had to balance out a range of claims. Because use of comparability has been fitful it has been associated with expensive 'catching-up' awards. There is no reason to suppose that the well-established pattern of intermittent recourse to comparability will be broken over the next decade; the only question is whether the use of the device will become more durable.

Future attempts are likely to follow the experience of the Comparability Commission in several respects. First, they are likely to see the advantage of having a body wholly concerned with the public services rather than, like the National Incomes Commission, the National Board for Prices and Incomes, and the Pay Board, trying to rule on market-oriented industries as well. Second, they will quickly discover that, in order to avoid destructive internal comparisons, the whole of the public services have to be treated as one. Third, that refined 'factor comparison' techniques have to be developed to permit comparisons for public sector jobs without external comparators. Fourth, that the different ethical values associated with public service, and the different career and supervisory practices, require considerable pioneering of techniques. Fifth, that this sort of pay fixing system will survive longer if the results of the enquiries are presented as material for negotiators rather than imposed as if binding arbitrations. The compatibility between this approach and that of 'informed collective bargaining' advocated by the recent Megaw Inquiry into civil service pay is particularly significant. Megaw noted the weakness of external market forces in the determination of pay, emphasising instead the managerial importance of internal wage structures and the potential they offer as devices for the motivation of employees.

However strong the arguments for a comprehensive approach to pay across all of government and public services, it is only likely to emerge, crabwise, from further expensive disputes. Governments will always be tempted to use pay restraint for public employees as an early and apparently easy means of restraining inflation. But, quite apart from the economic and political costs of the disputes themselves, it has already become evident that the bitterness of pay conflicts has a lasting effect in corroding the goodwill and co-operation upon which the efficient administration of government and public services depends. By effectively removing up to 5 million employees from the annual agony of pay settlement, a government would greatly ease its own task both as their ultimate employer and as manager of the economy.

Trade unions

Membership

Trade union membership has grown dramatically in recent years. Having been static since the Second World War, the proportion of the workforce in trade unions rose from 44 per cent in 1968 to 55 per cent in 1979. In the large food and drink and chemicals industries this growth was particularly rapid; in food and drink, for example, union density doubled over the period to attain 63 per cent in 1979. But in the past two years there has been an abrupt change. Union membership fell by one million members during 1980 and 1981 and union density declined to 52 per cent (Price and Bain, 1983). It is important to ask how far these losses simply reflect the fact that union members are losing their jobs, and how far they might indicate a wider retreat of trade unionism among the employed.

Certainly this happened between the two world wars, when overall union density fell from 45 per cent in 1920 to 23 per cent in 1932; this amounted to a net loss of nearly 4 million members while there were never more than 3 million registered unemployed and many of them had never been in unions. In some industries - agriculture, potteries, construction, chemicals, engineering and cotton - the fall was particularly dramatic, with the density of unionisation more than halving in the first three.

There are, however, good reasons for expecting union membership to be far less brittle in the 1980s. It is easy to forget how recent trade unionism was for most people in 1920; fewer than half of those in unions in that year could have been members five years earlier, and fewer than a quarter fifteen years earlier. Furthermore, sixty years later collective bargaining has become far more deeply embedded in the management process. Closed shops, most of them explicitly supported by management, cover approximately a half of trade union members. While we have no data to compare this with their pre-war extent, what has been notable about the recent spread of closed shops is that it has occurred most strongly outside their traditional (and shrinking) habitat of, for example, the metal working and printing industries. Comparing data from both the LSE and our own 1978 surveys with McCarthy's 1962 survey, it is apparent that the proportion of the labour force covered by closed shops rose from 4 per cent to 39 per cent in food, drink and tobacco, from 7 per cent to 32 per cent in chemicals, and from 6 per cent to 19 per cent in clothing and footwear, the majority of the growth occurring since 1970. The Department of Employment's 1980 survey of the tertiary sector suggests a similar growth of the closed shop in the private sector outside manufacturing, and in the public sector it covers the majority of the workforce (Hawes and Smith, 1981).

Probably as important in preventing a collapse of union membership among the employed in the 1980s is the widespread use of check-off arrangements. Almost universal in the public sector, and covering three-quarters of union members in manufacturing and a similar proportion in the larger tertiary establishments, this practice of management deducting members' union dues is likely to protect them from substantial erosion through disillusion or poverty. Most check-off arrangements came into existence in the 1970s and they have spread farthest in just those industries which have experienced the most recent increase in trade union density. However shallow the roots of the newly arrived unionism, it has strong protection from management.

Although the number of trade unions has continued a steady decline - from 543 in 1970 to 438 in 1980 - the distribution of the bulk of membership between the largest unions has barely altered. In 1970 the 40 unions with more than 50,000 members covered 85 per cent of all trade unionists; in 1980 the 39 unions of comparable size covered 87 per cent of unionists. The share of those with over a quarter of a million members rose from 55 to 60 per cent. Substantial change to this picture will come from the activities of the main predator unions, the TGWU, AUEW, GMWU and ASTMS. A recent study argues that they are unlikely to manage mergers among themselves but rather will search for 'minor partners, who can be more easily absorbed into an existing or barely modified government structure, in ways that are unlikely to threaten existing alliances and power groups' (Undy, Ellis, McCarthy and Halmos, 1981).

Organisation

The most striking development in trade union organisation since the war has been the rise in importance of the lay official. The move to single-employer bargaining in the private sector, and the reorganisations and use of incentive schemes in public employment, encouraged the emergence of the shop steward. Full employment gave workforces a confidence that permitted their stewards to operate without the fear of victimisation and dismissal that had been so great an inhibition in earlier decades. A crucial question for the 1980s is the extent to which high unemployment and changed management attitudes will erode the role of the shop steward.

Shop steward organisation had become extremely widespread by the end of the 1970s. The number of stewards increased from roughly 200,000 in the mid-1960s to roughly 300,000. In manufacturing, the largest tertiary establishments, and the public sector, managers reported there to be shop stewards for both manual and non-manual employees in almost every establishment where their respective unions were recognised. Some sort of senior steward was generally acknowledged for all but the smallest workforces. Of particular significance was the rise of the full-time shop steward, paid by management to attend to union duties throughout the week. The number of these officials in manufacturing quadrupled from the mid-1960s to between 4 and 5 thousand and substantial numbers were reported in the tertiary sector in 1980, most of whom had had their posts created in the previous four years. Clegg deduced that there may have been as many as 10 thousand full-time stewards in the whole of employment by the end of the 1970s, a number well over twice as great as that of full-time officials dependent on trade unions for their salaries (Clegg, 1979).

The apparently uniform advance of shop steward organisation over the past two decades is, however, misleading. First, it conceals marked variations in the character of the organisations. There is, for example, a very substantial difference between an experienced steward organisation in the engineering industry and a newly created one in a food factory in terms of their dependence on management, their range of bargaining, and the depth of support by the workforce. The organisations that sprang up in the 1970s with the full range of management-provided facilities may prove to be ineffective in the face of a managerial withdrawal from collective bargaining. There is already anecdotal evidence of the widespread withdrawal of that very management-dependent facility, the full-time shop stewardship.

Furthermore, the essentially workplace-based nature of shop steward strength is proving vulnerable to the increased tendency of management to raise the level of decision-making (if not of bargaining) away from the individual establishment. Combine committees of shop stewards, seeking to create unity of organisation across more than one factory in an enterprise, have found it difficult to mobilise sentiments of solidarity across their scattered memberships. This has, paradoxically, been especially so where traditions of workplace bargaining have been strongest; 'factory chauvinism' has obstructed company-wide unity. It has been easier for shop stewards to cope when the level of bargaining has been raised to that of the division or whole company. By effectively giving management recognition to the combine committee this reduces the sectional tendencies of individual factories. Even so, multi-unionism presents a serious obstacle to these efforts; corporate bargaining appears to proceed more smoothly where a single union is involved and where, in consequence, relationships between shop stewards and full-time officials are more clearly defined.

Two central problems for any trade union lie in the need to forge solidarity across a bargaining unit and to get the level of bargaining addressed to the level of management control. The magnitude of this organisational task was increased in the 1970s by the coincidence of greater shop steward activity at the workplace with increased government intervention. Most unions responded by increasing what Undy and his colleagues call the 'dispersal of decision-making' on bargaining matters. For the more decentralised unions this required little constitutional change; for the others such changes tended to be piecemeal and ad hoc. The decentralisation that was achieved in the bargaining field was generally not matched by any comparable decentralisation in non-bargaining matters, with the possible, and important, exception of the TGWU. There may thus be less difficulty than might be expected for unions in further adapting their decision-making procedures to the fundamentally changed labour market.

What new demands will be made on trade unions by heavy unemployment and changed management strategies? In the private sector we have argued that there is not likely to be a reversion to industry-wide, multi-employer bargaining. Instead companies will tend to pursue an 'ability to pay' policy, implying that they will seek to bargain for increased productivity at the level of individual establishments, shrug off pressures for comparability between establishments, and raise the level of control and strategic decision-making above the level of bargaining. The vigour with which they will do this, and the extent to which they will modify the form of collective bargaining, will depend upon questions of 'style' discussed earlier. In the public sector we have noted the tendency for greater control over effort levels and incentive schemes at the workplace and greater co-ordination of management at the national level.

On the union side, deepening unemployment is making a reliance upon fragmented, shop steward-led bargaining look increasingly inappropriate. Quite apart from the growing vulnerability of stewards to management hostility, there is Turner's observation that,

> other things being equal, the more decentralised the bargaining system, the faster wages are likely to move in whatever direction they are moving anyway. That is why national agreements were so important in the inter-war depressions; because they reacted less promptly than wage-rates determined at the workplace level, they set a 'floor' to the general tendency of wages to fall. (Turner, 1970)

As real wages tumble in erstwhile strongholds of shop steward power such as the engineering industry, the logic of the trade union need to build larger coalitions becomes ever more pressing.

The nature of such new coalitions is, however, far from clear. In the public sector the direction of current developments will tend to assist increased centralisation on the union side. But in the private sector developments will work against it, increasing the pressure on weakened workplace organisations and exacerbating sectional tendencies. If industry-wide agreements more or less held between the wars, it was in part because they offered a fall-back position following the progressive collapse of district agreements. For the modern private sector, dominated by large and sometimes multi-industry firms, there are few incentives to reconstruct industry-wide solidarity and, as we have noted, there is little sign of its being attempted. If wages were the principal bargaining issue then it might be practical for unions to seek to co-ordinate action on a company-by-company basis. But so long as redundancies remain a central concern there is little chance of this. Redundancy is a peculiarly corrosive issue for trade unions. It sets one factory up in competition with another in the same company in their struggle for survival. Within those factories, the ever-seductive individual lure of voluntary redundancy payments undermines collective resistance to job-shedding productivity schemes.

Although there may be few signs of it at present, these pressures point to a fundamental change in the style of trade union leadership. The rhetoric of rank-and-file action may increasingly be displaced by demands for centralised discipline. It is instructive to note that Ernest Bevin, who did as much as anyone to nurse collective bargaining through the last depression, wrote in 1924,

> Sectional stoppages must be discouraged. The experience of the Union during the past three years is that lightning strikes are the reverse of successful; ... that the cost

associated with same is very heavy; and that, following upon their termination, they invariably result in loss of prestige to the Union and loss of membership.

Strongly opposed to opportunism in wage negotiations, in 1929 he wrote, 'The trade unionist does not want to be always fighting for increased wages or resisting reductions; he wants stability so long as it is based upon a proper standard of living' (Allen, 1957). Even if arguments of collective strength did not point this way, the increased risk of fines under the Employment Acts and rapidly dwindling funds from membership loss would.

Above the level of individual unions, the prospects for the Trades Union Congress are uncertain. Having developed substantially since the 1960s, it now finds itself denied three crucial sources of authority. There is a government that feels no need to talk to it, even on questions of employment legislation. The CBI is not required by its members to engage in any substantial dealings with it. The Labour Party to which it is linked has bleaker electoral chances than at any time since the war. Of course these may not be enduring circumstances. An increase in the rate of price inflation, for example, could quickly renew tripartite activity. Developments in pay bargaining in the public sector are likely to encourage the TUC committees that seek to co-ordinate union responses; memories of the costs of the 1978-9 'winter of discontent' will provide a ready stimulus. But the authority of the TUC in private sector matters is, in the long run, unlikely to develop further than is permitted by the degree of unity of employers.

Conflict, control and co-ordination

Bearing the developments described in mind, it is possible to say something about three questions which unavoidably dominate discussion of the future of British industrial relations: What will happen to strikes? What will happen to management's control over work? What will happen to the fragmentation or co-ordination of bargaining?

Working days lost in stoppages, having been fairly stable through the 1960s, rose sharply in the early 1970s, fell erratically to a low level in 1976, and rose to a new peak in 1979, only to fall to a low level again in 1981. The pattern of days lost is dominated by relatively few large strikes. The sheer weight of numbers of employees for these means that they tend to occur where pay is determined through industry-wide agreements. The most powerful of these agreements are in the public sector (although engineering was important in 1979) and the increased propensity of public employees to take strike action in the 1970s, for reasons discussed earlier, lies behind these recent movements. Although there have been some large strikes in response to rationalisation - as in steel and railways - the principal cause has been breakdowns in public sector pay policy. We can thus say with some confidence that future loss in working days for all employees will be largely dependent upon the extent to which public employees can be reconciled to their pay fixing machinery.

The number of strikes recorded has, in contrast, remained remarkably steady at between 2 and 3 thousand per year for the last twenty-five years; it rose to 3,900 in 1970 and fell to 1,300 (in round numbers) in 1980 and 1981. Within these limits it has fluctuated in partial synchrony with the business cycle. It should be added that the industrial distribution of strikes has altered substantially, partly as a result of a combination of payment system reform and general contraction in coalmining, docks, shipbuilding and vehicles. It would be unsafe to assume that the continuation of high unemployment will necessarily mean a continuation of the low number of strikes. Employees may become to some extent inured to the level of unemployment and bottled-up grievances may break out with only a minor recovery. Furthermore, in relatively buoyant industries the argument that strikes lead to job loss may lose conviction and employees may take action to raise their pay up the industrial league table.

In the longer term there is likely to be a slow decline in the underlying trend of the number of strikes. Quite apart from the decline of some of the more strike-prone industries, the whole of manufacturing, which accounts for a disproportionate half of all strikes, has been contracting rapidly. While it is true that the past two decades have seen a willingness to strike spread to large sectors of the workforce for whom it had hitherto been almost unknown - women, white-collar workers, public services, and many private service industries - it is difficult to envisage their strike propensity ever approaching that of the miners, dockers and car workers who dominated the statistics in the 1960s. There are, however, sanctions other than strikes which are at least as common and which have comparable significance in terms of management control over the conduct of work (Edwards and Scullion, 1982). Overtime working is remarkably resilient in Britain. Between the end of 1980 and the end of 1982, despite a massive rise in unemployment, the proportion of manufacturing operatives who worked overtime remained at about 30 per cent and their average hours of overtime at about eight per week. The cheap and easy sanction of the overtime ban will be widely available for a long time to come.

What of the question of control? Will the 1980s see a 'new realism' in terms of an increased willingness to adopt more efficient working practices? There can be little doubt that century-old traditions of craft unionism and employer disunity have provided Britain with a form of collective bargaining that is distinctive in the extent to which it permits bargaining over the conduct of work at the workplace. Analysts of very varied persuasions are agreed that this provides employees in Britain with an internationally unusual ability to resist management attempts to raise effort, change working practices, or reduce real wages. There is thus broad agreement that worker resistance provides a constraint on Britain's international competitiveness, although opinions would differ on how central this was to the country's underlying economic problems. The impact of high unemployment on strike frequency may be of merely superficial significance by comparison with its impact upon this worker resistance and the basis of workplace union organisation.

There can be no doubt that major changes have been occurring in working practices during the past two years. Although there is no basis for quantifying them, and although there are some contrary cases of increased inflexibility of working, the weight of evidence is of widespread abandonment of restrictions, as well as of acceptance of real wage cuts. It would, however, be unwise to judge the durability of these changes in terms of some fundamental alteration in employee attitudes. Any 'new realism' is likely to be as ephemeral in the face of an economic recovery as were the attitudes of the 1930s when wartime restored job security. The permanence of the change depends upon management controls. We have argued that, well before the recent rise in unemployment, managements in both private and public sectors made substantial efforts to increase their controls over pay and the conduct of work. Furthermore, we have argued that there is likely to be a move towards a more 'consultative' style of management, reducing the scope for collective resistance to employer initiatives. It is where managements have adopted a 'pragmatic' style that their increased control over the conduct of work will not outlive a recovery in their product market position.

At least as important for Britain's international competitiveness as the question of control is that of the co-ordination of bargaining. In the 1960s and 1970s Britain's fragmented bargaining structure tended to amplify price inflation, whatever its origin, as separate groups outbid each other in an unguided effort to protect real wages. It was a major factor provoking direct government intervention in pay bargaining with all its consequential problems. In the 1980s the rise in unemployment has reduced the ability of workplace trade union organisations to pursue comparability claims and has thus caused the inflationary implications of fragmentation to recede. But an economic recovery would put to the test the effectiveness of both the control and the co-ordination of bargaining, and upon the outcome would depend to a large extent the chance of the recovery being sustained.

Part 2

A framework for analysis and an appraisal of main developments

Michael Poole

Introduction

The objective of this report is to examine, on the basis of sociological assumptions, and with special reference to management, the likely developments in British industrial relations in the forthcoming decade. During the past fifteen or so years, this aspect of our national life has of course had momentous economic, political and social repercussions for all members of the population and, as a consequence, it has been the focal point for a considerable measure of popular and scholarly disputation. Moreover, in view particularly of fundamental technical changes in manufacturing industry in the future, issues of labour-management relations are almost certain to feature no less prominently in these respects during the period under review. A project which is designed to highlight trends and movements in this context is thus potentially of substantial practical as well as academic import, with a series of far-reaching implications for policy.

The analysis itself begins in Section 1 by the delineation of an overall framework of analysis that comprises the main forces which have had a strategic impact upon Britain's patterns of industrial relations. Such a general mode of interpretation, however, in turn forms the prelude for the examination, in Section 2 of likely changes in the structure and policy of employers' associations and managers, of trade unions and of the legislature in the context of industrial relations. Finally, in Section 3, the implications for policy will be appraised by means of an analysis of those areas in which important initiatives are particularly likely.

A framework for analysis

The forces which bear upon any given national system of industrial relations are many and various. Nevertheless, in an attempt to simplify and to isolate the main factors involved in this context, we have attempted to classify the principal explanatory dimensions of industrial relations in Figure 2.1. As will be seen, these comprise certain strategic or deep-rooted elements in the wider environment of a given system of industrial relations (structural and subjective conditions); the institutional structure of industrial relations coupled with organisational factors at enterprise level; power and power conflicts between the main industrial relations groups; and the development, outcomes and practice of industrial relations. In Section 2 the latter elements in this framework will be appraised but the main changes in British society which are likely to affect labour-management relations in the period in focus should be examined at this juncture.

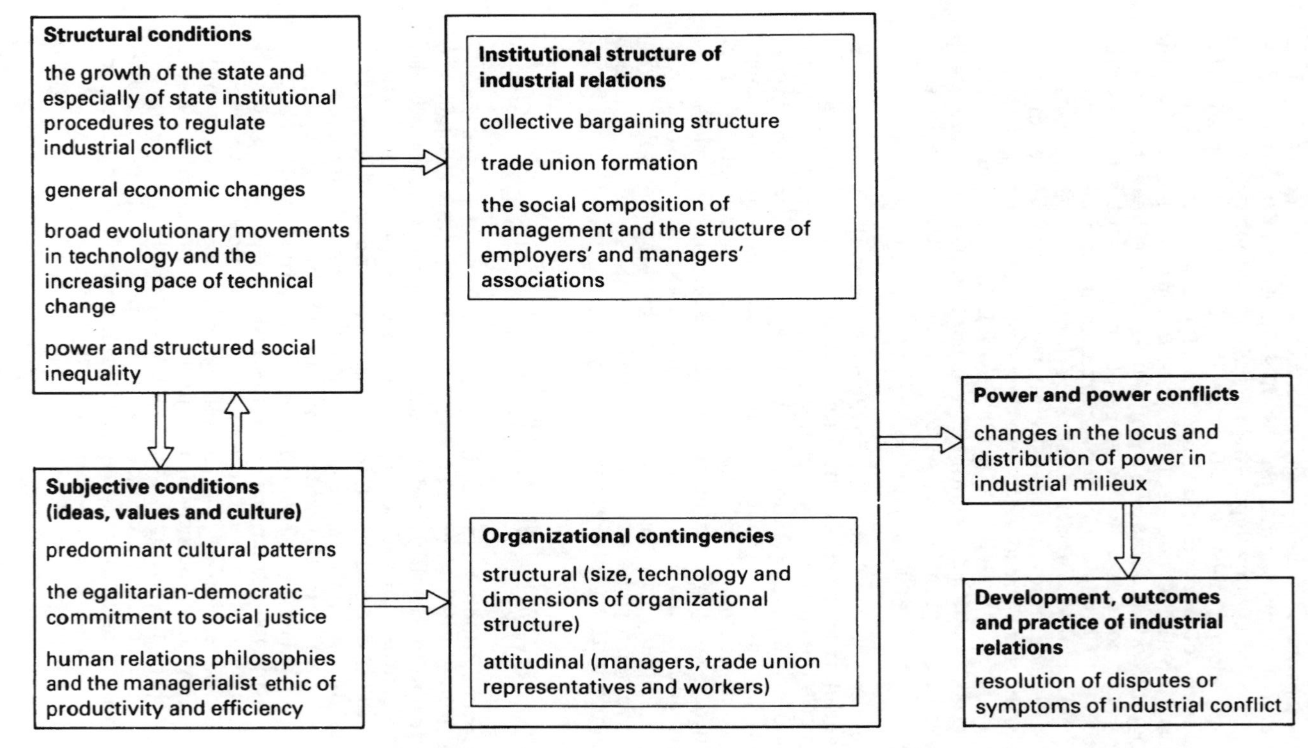

Figure 2.1 *Explanatory dimensions of industrial relations*

A framework for analysis and an appraisal of main developments

Structural conditions

The changing morphology of a country's pattern of industrial relations is thus influenced to begin with by certain independent general developments of a structural or strategic nature in the wider economic, political and social environment. In the case of Britain, there are four major principal forces of this type: the growth of the state and especially of legislative and institutional procedures to regulate industrial conflict; general economic changes; broad evolutionary movements in technology and an increasing pace of technical change; and alterations in the distribution of power in the wider society.

The state
An increasing intervention by the state in economic and industrial organisation has thus been a nearly universal characteristic of Western societies in the twentieth century and may well be a late-development effect in countries currently embarking upon strategic economic development (Dore, 1973). The growth of state involvement in these respects in Britain has taken two principal forms: the emergence of a series of government-initiated and legislative forays which have affected all main employing enterprises, and public ownership of a number of key industries and services. The first departure has been generally related to the so-called 'corporatist phenomenon' while the second stems logically from the particular mode of socialism envisaged by successive Labour administrations and which has been resorted to occasionally in situations of major crisis in particular industries by a number of Conservative governments. In so far as projections for the future are concerned, however, developments in these respects are compounded by the currently 'anti-corporatist' as well as 'anti-socialist' Conservative philosophy and by the emergence of the Liberal/Social Democratic Alliance which is likely to be conducive to corporatism but not to public ownership.

At a general level, therefore, the substantial increase in labour legislation in the 1960s and 1970s has been seen in some quarters to reflect the rise of an increasingly corporatist type of social and economic system. The most familiar definition of corporatism is that of Pahl and Winkler who described it as:

> A comprehensive economic system under which the state intensively channels predominantly private-owned business towards four goals, which have been increasingly explicit during the current economic crisis: order, unity, nationalism and success. (1974: 72)

Moreover, the industrial relations elements of a corporatist policy include: wage/salary control, prohibition of strikes and lockouts, compulsory arbitration and inquisitorial tribunals (investigating, for example, the causes of specific industrial disputes which have been officially outlawed).

The prospects of an evolution towards a corporatist type of industrial relations system in Britain involving a substantial measure of government intervention in the determination of both wages and salaries and the resolution of disputes have been the subject of considerable debate in the literature. At one level writers such as Pahl and Winkler regard such developments as to some extent a necessary outcome of attempts to solve Britain's perennial economic problems and, more specifically, to secure a measure of order in the employment relationship. On this view, then, the magnitude of the industrial and social restructuring which is now required in Britain coupled with the considerable expenditure involved in underwriting advanced technologies and ensuring success in economic resource allocation are such that control over industrial relations is almost certain to be a prime objective of any fully-fledged corporatist strategy. At the other extreme, however, there have been several commentators who have argued that the growth of state intervention is not the inevitable outcome of any long-term trend but rather has depended on a particular ideological development in industrial societies in the twentieth century. Thus Hayek in particular has seen such departures as in no way the inevitable concomitant of structural movements in society or of 'objective facts' beyond human control but rather as 'the product of opinions fostered and propagated for half a century till they have come to dominate all our policy' (1944: 32). But whatever the correct interpretation, the overall movement towards greater government involvement in labour-management relations is not in doubt and is manifested particularly in the considerable volume of legislation in this area in recent years.

Economic conditions

The patterns of industrial relations in Britain have historically been highly sensitive to certain strategic economic changes as well as to governmental initiatives. In an attempt to examine these effects in so far as the future is concerned, however, it is useful to begin our examination by reference to certain broad evolutionary changes in the economy in contemporary societies. This will be followed by a perusal of the more specific impress of employment concentration, inflation and unemployment on the patterns of labour relations.

The so-called post-industrial society is unlikely to have become fully characteristic of Britain in a decade or so hence. Nevertheless, the strategic trend in advanced industrial nations is typically in the direction of a gradual decline in the secondary (goods-producing or manufacturing sector) and of its replacement by the tertiary (services such as transportation and utilities), the quaternary (trade, finance, insurance, real estate) and the quinary sectors (health, education, research, government, recreation or leisure) (Bell, 1973). In detail, then, Kumar (1978: 197-8) has summarised these developments as follows:

> Specifically these are held to be changes in economic activities, such that the post-industrial society is not primarily a goods-producing but a service economy; changes in occupational structure, such that white-collar workers replace blue-collar workers as the single largest category in the labour force, and within the white-collar category, there is an increasing predominance of the professional, scientific, and technical groups; and changes in the form of technology, with the older machine technology supplemented by the rise of the new 'intellectual technology' ... essentially management and problem-solving systems making extensive use of the computer, such as information theory, game theory etc. and which allow for rational planning, prediction, monitoring, and self-sustaining technical growth in all areas of the society.

In Britain the trend away from manufacturing has been substantially accelerated in recent years by a considerable degree of de-industrialisation occasioned by high exchange and interest rates and by other fiscal and taxation policies which have had a particularly damaging effect on this sector of the economy. The balance of payments problems which would normally accompany such a departure have been more than offset by the favourable counterbalancing financial effects of North Sea oil but the upshot has of course been a substantial rise in unemployment to levels unknown since the 1930s. Nevertheless, in so far as the strategic changes in occupations accompanying such a movement are concerned, the trend towards a 'post-industrial society' has clearly been accelerated recently, albeit in a rather distorted and truncated form. That is to say, although service and leisure industries, health and government modes of employment and so on have become increasingly important parts of the overall economy, they have not necessarily evolved organically on the basis of an advanced technological manufacturing base, but rather have remained less seriously affected by the exigencies of the economic stagnation of the early 1980s.

The industrial relations consequences of the gradual change from manufacturing industry to services and other similar types of occupation are undoubtedly profound. This is particularly manifested in trade union structure since those organisations confined to recruitment in traditional heavy sectors of industry necessarily decline vis-à-vis those which have constituencies specifically adapted to the emergent modes of employment. The establishment of new industries, too, provides a favourable basis for the implementation of fresh managerial initiatives in labour relations. Moreover, the social composition of trade unions typically changes because the 'post-industrial' varieties of employment are far more likely to contain a substantial number of female employees than is the case in traditional manufacturing enterprises. Again, such a background is conducive to the establishment of procedural and substantive agreements which are unencumbered by customs and practices which, in certain cases, have their origins in upwards of a century of management-union negotiations.

Turning more specifically, then, to the effects of employment concentration, inflation and unemployment on labour relations, these have historically been substantial, but the trends in each respective dimension are by no means easy to predict with any reasonable degree of accuracy over the next ten years. Taking first of all, then, employment concentration, the hundred largest manufacturing firms had an average employment of 20,300 in 1958, a figure which mounted to 31,180 in 1972 and British manufacturing firms (as distinct from establishments) tend to be unusually large by comparison with other European countries (Prais, 1976: 62; Hannah and Kay, 1977: 120). Moreover, the effects of size of enterprise on trade union density, strikes, absenteeism, labour turnover, the 'formalisation' of procedures for handling disputes and the growth of shop stewards' committees and other plant-based organisations of labour have been demonstrated in a wide range of separate studies (Ingham, 1970; Brown et al., 1978; Bain, 1970; Brown, 1981; Boraston, Clegg and Rimmer, 1975).

It is likely, however, that an overall increase in employment concentration would produce in its train a further growth in union density and union organisation, an expansion of formal, managerially initiated procedures for resolving industrial disputes and a further upsurge of strike activity and other symptoms of disharmony such as absenteeism and labour turnover. However, such developments may well be counterbalanced by the rather different effects of unemployment, by the pressure from various quarters to reap the considerable social benefits of small-scale enterprise, and by the emergence of a series of locally based enterprises stimulated partly as a means of resolving unemployment problems and partly as a logical consequence of the trend towards a 'post-industrial society' which we have just described.

In so far as the ramifications of inflation for industrial relations are concerned these again have been subject to detailed investigation (cf. Bain and Elsheikh, 1976; Price and Bain, 1976). Indeed, inflation is almost certainly conducive to trade union growth and to an upsurge of industrial militancy. Hence, on the basis of the econometric model of union growth by Bain and Elsheikh, rates of changes of pay and prices were found to have been highly significant determinants of union growth in Britain in the period since 1892. Nevertheless, the impact of rising prices would appear to be less influential above a rate of 4 per cent a year and can be offset by unemployment, which can obviously have a significant negative effect on union growth. Moreover, in so far as the dynamics of this process are concerned, Price and Bain have noted how the 'threat effect' of high inflation on living standards tends to encourage employees to join trade unions in increasing numbers and, at the same time, the ability of a given union to maintain members' real incomes in such a situation results in the so-called 'credit-effect' of a positive commitment by the membership to the union itself (Price and Bain, 1976). Again, it is worth emphasising that inflation tends to be experienced universally amongst all employees in a given population regardless of whether they are of salaried or of wage-earning status. This, then, can result in widespread industrial unrest and the willingness to consider militant tactics amongst groups for whom the very principle of collective action would once have been abjured.

The impact of unemployment on industrial relations has clearly become an issue of considerable moment in the early 1980s. Furthermore, notwithstanding the fact that unemployment benefits are on a considerably more generous scale than in the 1930s, the typical effects would appear to be to discourage union growth and union militancy, to result in renewed attempts by management to reassert control over the production process and to reduce the expectations of the workforce for autonomy and freedom on the job and for participation in decision-making processes in the enterprise.

The principal effect of unemployment in the context of industrial relations is thus to alter the balance of power in the organisation and to diminish the horizons of those in subordinate roles who remain in work. The first is manifested in a decline in union density (cf. Bain and Elsheikh, 1976) and the second in a reduction in union militancy and employee expectations and a more aggressive managerial posture in so far as the establishment of pay targets and the day-to-day processes of decision-making in the workplace are concerned. Amongst the unemployed themselves the typical experience would still appear to be one of 'shock-optimism-pessimism-fatalism' even though, as Sinfield has remarked, this hypothesis has generally been illustrated and supported rather than tested and validated (Sinfield, 1981: 37). But gradually such experiences tend to filter through to those in work who become more likely to accept without demur workplace practices which, in conditions of full employment, would have been systematically opposed.

Nevertheless, the situation of high unemployment in the 1980s may well be historically unique not only in terms of the less serious economic consequences for individual families than was the case in the 1930s but more especially in terms of the so-called 'ideology of work' itself (Anthony, 1977). That is to say, to the extent that work for previous generations represented a calling and a duty and its loss had perforce the most serious of social and psychological consequences for the individuals concerned, there is increasing evidence to suggest that modern attitudes to work may have undergone a considerable transformation since the Second World War. More specifically, too, there has been a growth in the informal economy and to some extent a reduction in the division between home and work and in unpaid and paid wage labour (Gershuny and Pahl, 1980), all of which may be both a cause and consequence of different attitudes to employment in the modern era. Again, to the extent that such an inference is valid, it may be that the well-rehearsed effects of unemployment on labour relations highlighted in the foregoing may prove to be substantially less marked than in previous eras.

At the same time, however, the prospects for employment in the 1980s are undoubtedly bleak unless a substantial change in economic and political policy occurs in the meantime. In November 1981, The National Institute of Economic and Social Research produced a figure of 3.4 million unemployed by 1986 (NIESR, 1981: 18). But in February 1982, the short-term estimate of this body for unemployment in 1983 had already risen from 3.1 million, in November 1981, to 3.3 million (NIESR, 1982: 15) and hence a corresponding adjustment of the 1986 projection to at least 3.6 million would seem to be reasonable. Meanwhile, in their 1981 Economic Review, the Cambridge Economic Policy Group estimated that unemployment would be nearly 4.5 million by the mid-1980s ('Financial Times', 1981a). Moreover, when to the effects of economic policy are added various likely technological implications for unemployment, the chances of continuing to maintain employment in the traditional manner are almost certainly limited. But for these and other reasons, it seems highly probable that some more fundamental change in the conception of work and leisure and in the meaning of gainful employment will be manifest by the end of the decade. After all, even quite massive investments in industry would not provide enough employment to solve a problem of this magnitude and would in some respects run counter to the long-term trends in industrial societies and to the physical limits to growth which have been outlined in a number of studies of the future (see, for example, The Club of Rome Report, 1975).

Technology

Turning, then, to examine the likely effects of technical change on industrial relations involves the consideration of a wide-ranging and interesting (if, at times, highly speculative) literature. It is our considered view, however, that it is easier to underestimate the impact of technology on work roles and relationships than to overstate its probable influence in the next decade. After all, we are currently experiencing a technological revolution which is no less fundamental in its ramifications for the occupational structure in Britain than the advent of industry itself in the latter part of the eighteenth century. In order to make some sense of the existing debates our examination of the influence of technology on industrial relations begins by a consideration of the so-called 'technical implications school', with special reference to the role of automation. This is followed by a review of some more imaginative contributions from writers who have taken cognisance of the micro-electronics revolution, the effects of which are likely to become increasingly profound over the next ten years.

In classical industrial sociological literature a series of contributions related the extent to which the technical organisation of work could have far-reaching implications for patterns of human organisation in the enterprise (Blauner, 1964; Woodward, 1965; Touraine, 1965). The most significant proposition was founded on the concept of the technical scale, which implied a gradual movement from craft forms of production, through various intermediary machine-tending and mass production types, to fully automated or process enterprises. Moreover, on this view, there were likely to be profound consequences of this change for industrial relations. Thus for Blauner, the intermediary ranges of technology (especially in mass production, car assembly plants) had the most dissatisfying modes of work environment and hence were conducive to considerable management-worker hostility, while in automated factories based on continuous-process technology, the workers' sense of control over the work process was restored. That is to say, continuous-process technology offered more scope for 'self-actualisation' than machine and assembly-line technologies. The nature of the work encouraged a scientific, technical orientation and the changing character of technology resulted in opportunities for learning and personal development for a considerable section of the blue-collar labour force (Blauner, 1964: 174). In such a milieu, too, it was not unreasonable to suppose that industrial relations would be far more harmonious than in the intermediary types of technological environment. Moreover, although this view has been challenged (Braverman, 1974; Wood, 1982), the impact of technical change on industrial relations has proved to be a fruitful area for research (see, for example, Martin, 1981).

Nevertheless, a concern over the implications of technology for the evolution of modern societies and for the patterns of control, authority and administration in contemporary and future social orders has a wide and impressive ancestry in the annals of the social sciences. Moreover, if we turn our attention to examine the likely implications of the micro-electronic revolution for industrial relations in the next decade, a passage from a recent conference organised by the Organisation for Economic Co-operation and Development is worth quoting:

> There can be no doubt ... that the major technological development today is in the field of microelectronics and the related areas of information, computers and communications ... the development of microelectronics presents a number of unique characteristics which have virtually no precedent in the history of technology. Since microelectronic technology can perform a large variety of tasks involving the production or collection, manipulation, and transmission of information its field of application is very wide. Applications range from aerospace to military products, capital goods, and consumer products to the automation and control of industrial processes, transportation systems and office functions.... The impact of microelectronics is heightened by the convergence of other technological developments interacting with it, such as lasers, optical fibres, printing and display technologies, software, automation, telecommunications and so forth. (Kendrick, 1981: 264)

But what it may be reasonably asked are the likely consequences of so profound a technological change for patterns of industrial relations in the enterprise? Since the probable effects are multi-faceted and very broad in compass it is worth summarising the key trends in the following form (see for a detailed account OECD, 1981; Jenkins and Sherman, 1979).

(1) The effects of micro-electronics are likely to be fundamental in terms of the structure of employment, the nature of jobs and quality of working life and on socio-economic institutions and practices generally.

(2) In so far as the changes in employment are concerned, in manufacturing there is likely to be increased employment in design and development and sales and maintenance with fewer opportunities in the production of final goods and of parts. More generally, too, there will be a shift from non-information

to information occupations (e.g. managers, scientists and computer analysts) (OECD, 1981).

(3) Nevertheless, the overall employment effects of such a change have not been agreed upon amongst leading commentators. At one extreme, Jenkins and Sherman have argued that 'remain as we are, reject the new technologies and we face unemployment of up to 5.5 million by the end of the century. Embrace the new technologies, accept the challenge and we end up with unemployment of 5 million.' (Jenkins and Sherman, 1979: 113). Yet, in other accounts, it has been observed that high technology industries create more employment opportunities than low technology industries, while the supporting infrastructure of education, training and retraining which is required results in an expansion of jobs in the 'knowledge field' (OECD, 1981).

(4) Eventually the computer-integrated automated factory and the automated office will be realised although this may not be evident in Britain in ten years' time. But while a certain amount of decentralisation of control is occasioned by the new technology, the predominant impact of microprocessor electronic digital technology is to reduce discretion in work functions and to increase centralisation. As the OECD report points out, although the interest of the work may be enhanced, so also is stress and possibly alienation from work. Hence, even though the new technologies will contribute to greater abundance, they will not create equity in themselves (OECD, 1981: 269).

(5) Indeed, in so far as the quality of working life is concerned, jobs will become increasingly demanding mentally but less demanding physically. Again, there are strong prospects that employment will increase for professional and skilled workers but that other types of occupation will be deskilled, made more routine and even, as we have observed, eliminated entirely. This may create an increasing polarisation in work between the qualified and unqualified and the educated and less-educated as opposed to the skilled and unskilled in a conventional sense.

(6) The effects of these changes in the trade unions are also very interesting since clearly the trend towards white-collar, professional and managerial unionism at the expense of trade unionism amongst traditional manual workers can only be further exacerbated. The official view of the Trade Union Advisory Committee (TUAC) to the OECD is that trade union participation should be encouraged in the formative stages of decision-making in this context at enterprise, industry, national and international levels; that the growth of the electronic sectors should be 'planned, balanced and accountable';

that corresponding policies of qualitative and quantitative growth (especially in the service sector) should be pursued; that increased leisure and reduced working time should be logical accompaniments of this movement; and that rapid adjustments in the labour market (especially in training and retraining) should be a major objective (OECD, 1981: 272). Similarly, as part of the day-to-day consultative process, it has been suggested that employees should elect special representatives ('data shop stewards') to represent them in the processes of decision-making.

(7) Finally, with respect to the employment opportunities for women, although in some types of production occasioned by the new technology the dominant group will be female, at the same time it has been observed that some of the jobs most at risk from the micro-electronic revolution are now largely performed by women. Hence, drawing on Australian data, Smith has noted that over 50 per cent of the female workforce is 'employed in occupations that are in risk of significant labour displacement' as opposed to only 25 per cent of the male workforce. Hence it may well be the case that 'women will disproportionately bear the burden of job displacement imposed by the widespread adoption of the new technology' (Smith, 1981: 241).

Power and structured social inequality

No sociological analysis of the general factors affecting industrial relations and the likely course of their development over the next decade, however, could afford to ignore a consideration of the impress of the distribution of power in the wider society on the emergent pattern. After all, in a series of writings, the specific problems of trade union-management relationships have been traced, at least in part, to structured social inequalities at this level (Fox, 1974; Goldthorpe, 1974; Hyman, 1975). Moreover, in analytical terms, Dunlop (1958) has viewed the distribution of power in 'the larger society' as a crucial factor bearing upon labour relations, while even critics of the 'social stratification thesis' in so far as trade union growth and character are concerned have acknowledged the significance of power in this particular context (Bain, Coates and Ellis, 1973).

For much of the period since the Second World War, then, there was no doubt that power in British society shifted to some extent away from employers and towards organised labour. This was particularly obvious when set against the situation of declining trade union membership in the early part of the 1930s and the very weakened position of the labour force as a whole after the demise of the General Strike in 1926. The causes of this change have been complex but there was little doubt that full employment, the welfare measures introduced particularly by the Labour administration of 1945-51, changing social attitudes (occasioned largely by the upheavals of the two world wars) manifested in an unwillingness to accept established institutions and managerial decision-making prerogatives, the strength of what the Webbs (1897) once termed 'the democratic current', and technical innovations which disrupted social hierarchies in the workplace were of signal importance in this respect.

Such wider economic, political and social changes thus provided strategic power resources for the trade unions which, particularly in the 1970s, enjoyed a period of influence over government that has no obvious historical parallel. In the 1980s, however, the situation began to alter again for with rising unemployment and the particular threats to jobs in manufacturing industry, a cornerstone of labour power in the post-war period had been undermined. Moreover, the increased public hostility to trade unions not only provided a basis for the enactment of legislation which has been explicitly designed to curtail certain militant tactics but also enabled managers to make a series of direct appeals to the workforce without embarking upon prior consultations through trade union channels. In so far as the situation over the next decade or so is concerned, the considerable historical shifts in the power of labour imply that there is no necessary evolutionary trend of a type which would make prediction reasonably straightforward. If unemployment remains high over the period in question, however, it does seem likely that a series of restrictive labour laws will be enacted, that union influence at a strategic level over governments will continue to diminish, and that a series of managerial forays in labour and personnel policy will be mounted. However, it is likely that certain strategically placed groups of workers (for example in the energy context) will remain influential and could well have an impact on political policy no less consequential than that of the miners in 1972 and 1974.

Subjective conditions

The patterns of industrial relations in a given nation are also significantly affected by forces of a subjective character, notably by the wider culture and by the values and ideas which shape the attitudes and beliefs of management, trade unionists and members of governments in this area. This situation is manifested in the substantial variations in labour relations in countries with roughly similar politico-economic systems and experiencing equivalent rates and types of technical change. In order to evaluate these effects systematically, and to draw appropriate inferences for the future, the concept of culture and its impact on Britain's industrial relations is first discussed. This is followed by an analysis of the role of values and ideas in governmental policy, the attitudes of leading trade unionists and of managerial approaches to personnel and industrial relations questions.

Culture

In his classical definition, Tylor viewed culture as 'that complex whole which includes knowledge, belief, art, morals, law, custom and any other capabilities and habits acquired by man as a member of society' (Tylor, 1871: 1). However, in the context of industrial relations, the notion of institutional values (or those sets of beliefs which are transmitted through social institutions) is preferable to such a broad encompassing conception (cf. Child, 1981).

The most important single culture-effect has been the so-called 'tradition of voluntarism' which, until comparatively recently, has characterised Britain's overall system of industrial relations. Thus, as Allan Flanders noted, voluntarism is a complex pattern of beliefs with at least three principles (Flanders, 1970: 289).

> The first expresses a preference for collective bargaining over state regulation as alternative methods of settling wages and working conditions. The second favours keeping industrial disputes out of the courts by preserving our non-legalistic type of collective bargaining. The third principle is an insistence by the bargaining parties on their complete autonomy (the notion of 'free' collective bargaining) which leads them to resent any intervention in their affairs.

It is important to recognise, however, that all these principles have been eroded in recent British industrial relations history and it is likely that some further movement towards a legally based system of industrial relations will take place in the decade ahead. To be sure, the Industrial Relations Act of 1971 proved to be abortive but the strength of the 'corporatist current' coupled with public pressure is likely to result in further changes in this respect in the next ten years.

Values and ideas

There are, however, many other types of values and ideas which will influence the shape of Britain's industrial relations in future years. The growing role of the state in British society, for example, is likely to encourage an increasing concern for the so-called 'problem of order' in employment relationships and to result in attempts to produce so-called 'system integration' in this particular sphere. Moreover, members of the labour movement have been progressively influenced by egalitarian-democratic ideas and management by professionalism as well as by human relations philosophies.

In the first place, therefore, members of governments tend to view themselves as custodians of the national interest and to view any major dislocations in society with considerable circumspection. Threats to the social order that are seen to stem from protracted strikes or rising trends in strike activity thus become a source of considerable concern. The proposed solutions to these dilemmas will vary, of course, but the upshot is almost invariably to favour initiatives which are designed to bring about 'system integration' or the linking of various disparate bodies and organisations into some over-arching institutions subjected to persuasion by government and to legislative checks. Of course, even under a largely voluntarist system, governments have never abstained from intervention in labour disputes (quite extensive conciliation, mediation and arbitration machinery, for example, had been installed even before the establishment of the Advisory, Conciliation and Arbitration Service (ACAS)). Hence, if the state becomes more powerful in the next decade, as we have already observed it is likely to do, some movement towards more compulsory types of arbitration, towards attempts to outlaw a range of strikes until various third party institutions have been fully used, and towards the investigation of particular disputes by government officers may well become manifest.

Since the late 1960s, too, the labour movement has been much influenced by a range of egalitarian-democratic ideas. The origins of this development are by no means easy to trace but such a trend has become evident in the increasingly comprehensive blueprints for a radical reconstruction of British society and in the attempt to produce an 'irreversible' shift in wealth and power away from employers and towards working people and their families. Moreover, in the industrial relations context, the principal consequences of the implementation of such a policy would be a major change in the distribution of rewards in the workplace involving a considerable narrowing of pay differentials between management and employees (and amongst different groups of employees themselves) and also a fundamental shift in the patterns of decision-making in the enterprise by means of the development of industrial democracy machinery (in the form of participation by trade union activists in decision-making processes at board level).

But the values which inform managerial strategies in labour relations have also been transformed in the twentieth century. Thus, as Bendix observed, the original practices and ideologies of management were the consequence of an 'effort to promote industry in a relatively hostile environment' (Bendix, 1956: 6). The earliest entrepreneurial ideologies had been focused on self-interest as a legitimation of the 'quest for material advantage, social prestige and political participation' but, in Bendix's view, the separation of the functions of ownership and control resulted in attempts to emphasise a concept of work organisation which not only sanctioned managerial control over decision-making but also was designed to enlist the areas in which 'subordinates exercise their judgement' for managerial ends (Bendix, 1956: 251). The focus on control, however, can only be sustained in the long term by the development of professionalism and professional standards and by increasing sophistication in industrial relations and personnel policy. Hence it is scarcely surprising that managers have increasingly claimed professional status and have been concerned for both productivity and efficiency in the enterprise and for the establishment of effective personnel and employee relations functions within management itself. Moreover, although some of the more detailed strategies in this area will be examined later in Section 2, it is worth noting at this point that sophisticated 'human resourcing' and labour relations policies are likely to stem from widespread concern for professionalism and from the attempts by management to ensure effective control over labour in the years ahead.

Changes in management, in the trade unions and in legislation

So far, then, we have examined some of the broad forces which shape patterns of industrial relations with a view to setting out the main changes which are likely to affect labour-management relations in the forthcoming decade. In this section our discussions will be more specific and, above all, will serve to highlight probable developments in employers' associations and management, in trade union growth, structure and policy, and in legislation. This will also provide us with the opportunity to examine other fundamental dimensions of the explanatory framework including the institutional structure of industrial relations, organisational contingencies and power conflicts in the bargaining relationship and to show how these relate with the general forces for change outlined in the foregoing section.

Employers' associations and management

It is a familiar lament in the literature that British industrial relations scholars have concentrated their attention rather one-sidedly on the trade unions, with the result that current knowledge of employers' associations and of management is far from systematic and comprehensive. Moreover, although this state of affairs is gradually being remedied, the lack of detailed information applies particularly to the crucial area of managerial strategies in industrial relations. For the purposes of this review, it is useful to set out the available material under the three heads of the general forces affecting employer and managerial roles in industrial relations, ongoing trends and future predictions.

There are almost certainly four main groups of factors which influence the industrial relations conduct of employers' and managers: (1) external or environmental constraints (including various politico-economic conditions, rationality and culture); (2) managerial organisational structures within the enterprise and the institutional structure of industrial relations; (3) the attitudes and choices of managers themselves; and (4) the relative power of managers vis-à-vis the state and the trade unions.

In the first place, therefore, the role of employers and managers in industrial relations are shaped by a series of external characteristics of the wider organisational environment. Above all, then, the extent to which the relationships between enterprise and government are based on market principles, or on state intervention in a privately owned economic system (i.e. corporatism), or on public ownership and control has far-reaching implications for managerial strategies in the labour relations area. Broadly speaking, however, managerial initiatives in labour relations are most likely to take place where the role of the state is circumscribed, where the power of labour has not been destroyed by the ravages of unemployment and where inflation is not at a level which ensures a preoccupation with financial considerations. It is widely accepted, too, that the growth of the managerial group in modern societies and its increasing professionalism reflect trends to rationalisation in advanced industrial countries (cf. Weber, 1968). This, too, is likely to be demonstrated in increasing specialisation of managerial activities in labour relations, greater sophistication of personnel policy and the desire for formal procedures for resolving domestic disputes. However, the pattern is also affected by wider cultural and ideological forces; a situation which is indicated by international variations in managerial practices such as the British concern for a semi-constitutional strategy (involving consultation with and the recognition of trade unions) and the preference of French employers for paternalism, individualism and legalism (Gallie, 1978).

Organisational and institutional variables would also appear to be related to employer and managerial responses and the outcomes of industrial relations. For example, Turner et al. (1977) discovered that structures of management organisation affected propensity to strike in the enterprises covered in their investigation. Indeed, the incidence of strike activity was found to be positively correlated with 'standardization' and 'formalization' in general management and especially with the 'formalization of industrial relations' and 'facilities for shop stewards' (Turner et al., 1977: 72). By the same token, too, Clegg has observed that the institutional structure of collective bargaining was in part shaped by 'employers' organizations and managerial structure coupled with attitudes among employers' (1976: 10). More specifically, then, the trend to large-scale bureaucratic organisation tends to produce a corresponding growth in trade union activity, an increasingly formal character of that role within the workplace and a higher level of industrial conflict. And again, the movement to single-employer collective bargaining agreements in the 1970s has been very much a product of managerial strategies in the labour relations sphere.

Nevertheless, there is still a measure of choice in the selection of particular managerial styles and, in this respect, variations in attitudes of the managers themselves may be of considerable importance. For this reason, too, it is scarcely surprising that managerial practices are by no means uniform in British enterprises. At the same time, however, the capacity to develop and implement specific industrial relations strategies clearly reflects the power of the main parties in the overall system itself. A strong presence of the state thus tends to produce a highly legalised framework for union-management relations, while influential trade unions (and particularly plant-based representatives) are usually able to nullify or to reduce the practical effectiveness of particular managerial initiatives with which they have little sympathy.

But what, it may reasonably be asked, have been the dominant trends in employer and managerial roles in industrial relations in recent years? The main changes may be summarised under the following six points.

(1) The role of employers' associations in collective bargaining has continued to decline relatively to that of management but their advisory functions in industrial relations have substantially increased.

(2) Managers have potentially three rather different sources of loyalty (to the employer, to the professional managerial group and to the employees). In general, however, the commitment to the employing organisation and to market principles appears to be strong but this has been considerably enhanced by an increasing professional consciousness and by a greater willingness to join professional managerial bodies such as the British Institute of Management and the Institute of Personnel Management.

(3) There has been a marked specialisation in the industrial relations function of management in the last decade.

(4) The importance of personnel management in the overall priorities of the enterprise has also expanded over the same period.

(5) Procedures for dealing with domestic disputes and grievances have been developed at enterprise level and, as we have already seen, the local organisations of shop stewards have been encouraged in many British firms. At the same time, however, only a minority of managers are involved in formal collective bargaining in the plant.

(6) In so far as attitudes are concerned, managers would appear to be hostile to trade unions and against board-level types of employee participation. However, they favour the development of consultative procedures and the provision of more information to employees. They also endorse state involvement in certain selective industrial relations areas and support the current Conservative government's policies on secret ballots, secondary picketing and the closed shop.

Taking first of all, then, the role of employers' associations, it is of course possible to trace a major shift in their role in industrial relations since the nineteenth century when they were pre-eminent in the collective regulation of pay and conditions (Clegg, 1979: 62-123). A major change from this situation has been further exacerbated in the past decade by the tendency towards single-employer bargaining. Moreover, the principal reason for this modification has been the growth of managerial influence over industrial relations. At the same time, the majority of industrial manufacturing establishments appear to be affiliated either directly or indirectly to the Confederation of British Industry, the advisory role of employers' associations seems to have expanded in conjunction with increased government intervention in industrial relations, and multi-employer bargaining (particularly in areas of manufacture with low capital requirements and high ease of entry) still remains of primary importance for about a quarter of the manual workforce in British manufacturing industry (Brown, 1981: 5-25).

In so far as the managers themselves are concerned, it is possible to understand their role in industrial relations from three rather different points of view (as representatives of employers, as a distinctive professional group and as employees in the enterprise). The evidence from a recent survey of members of the British Institute of Management suggests that the first consideration is still uppermost as a source of identity for the modern executive but that an increasing professionalism and professional consciousness has become apparent (Mansfield et al., 1981; Poole et al., 1981). Moreover, the increasing importance of management associations such as the BIM has also been evident as has been the particular growth of specialist personnel bodies. Thus, between 1959 and 1979, membership of the Institute of Personnel Management virtually quadrupled from 4,308 to 20,194 members and it doubled in the ten years between 1969 and 1979 (Thomason, 1980: 34).

The expansion of single-employer bargaining has also brought in its train a considerable specialisation of the industrial relations function of management (Brown, 1981). Nevertheless, the decision to appoint specialist industrial relations management should not be seen as a straightforward response to the exigencies of a change in the structure of collective bargaining since, as the Warwick researchers also revealed, size of firm, preference for a further managerial division of labour and 'the decision to conduct bargaining within the company and at a level higher than the industrial establishment' were also found to be important considerations (Brown, 1981: 31).

In recent years, a great deal of attention has also been focused on the status of personnel and industrial relations officers in the overall management hierarchy (Ritzer and Trice, 1969; Watson, 1977; Legge, 1978). Moreover, as Clegg has observed, the salaries of personnel managers now run to well up amongst the specialist groups in British management (1979: 128). However, evidence from the recent Warwick survey indicates that the influence of personnel and industrial relations officers varies with the issues concerned being quite substantial for terms and conditions of employment and redundancy but of less importance in decisions on capital investments and major changes in production methods (Brown, 1981: 41).

Moreover, although, as we have already noted, in the 1970s managers at enterprise and company level clearly presided over a major extension of procedures for dealing with domestic disputes and grievances and in their attempts to make arrangements increasingly formal encouraged a rapid increase in the number of full-time shop stewards, it would erroneous to suggest that the majority of British managers are involved in formal collective bargaining. Indeed, evidence from the British Institute of Management survey indicated that, in 1980, only about 20 per cent of managers were implicated in formal collective bargaining (Mansfield et al., 1981; Poole et al., 1981).

Turning, then, to trends in managerial attitudes to industrial relations, there would seem to be considerable opposition to trade union power in modern Britain and to radical proposals for industrial democracy (such as worker directors being elected through trade unions). Moreover, although managers are generally against state intervention in industry and the economy, they tend to agree with certain types of industrial relations legislation (for example, on secret ballots, control of secondary picketing and changes in the effect of closed shop agreements). However, contemporary managers would appear to favour the provision of information to employees and joint consultation (Mansfield et al., 1981; Poole et al., 1981).

Future projections for the roles of employers and managers in industrial relations must, however, involve an imaginative extension of recent trends in a context of a rapidly changing political and economic climate and an awareness of further possible influences on the evolving patterns themselves (cf. Poole and Mansfield, 1980: 137-41). Moreover, although the situation of employers' associations may not alter dramatically (unless they become enmeshed in a series of planning bodies as part of a developing corporatist strategy), there could be a number of interesting changes in managerial strategies in labour relations in the forthcoming decade that are worth pursuing in greater detail.

It is in our view probable, then, that the trend towards a professional and collectively organised management is likely to continue even though this may take place in conjunction with the pursuit of a number of career and leisure projects. Certainly, the conditions which have facilitated such changes show no obvious signs of abating even though various pressures for managerial unionism (such as from the Bullock recommendations on industrial democracy) have become less intense. But equally, the growing concern over professional status is a durable phenomenon which is consistent with international movements in this respect and which has been augmented by the plethora of courses and programmes in management education.

At the same time, the industrial relations strategies of managers are liable to become increasingly sophisticated in design, comprehensive and formal in scope and to be informed by the input of knowledge from a variety of 'behavioural science' disciplines. Such a prognosis is based upon the persistence of acute problems on the labour relations front occasioned not least by the technical and economic upheavals which, in some form or another, can be expected to continue in the coming years. Indeed, further strains upon the social fabric and upon relationships within industrial milieux may well intensify and lend further support to these rapidly expanding movements.

Such tendencies, moreover, could be exacerbated by the trend towards an international dimension in industrial relations initiatives. Certainly, European legislation (from both the

Commission and the European Parliament) may well feature prominently in future management programmes and, in particular, may be a source for extensive changes in employee participation in British enterprises. Furthermore, an expanding role for the legislature (even if this is reflected in abrupt changes in party political philosophy) could be associated with the absorption of an increasing amount of managerial time in interpreting the requirements and stipulations of the respective enactments and may well further enhance the advisory functions of employers' associations.

Alterations in legislation and in industrial relations strategy may also be the prelude for significant modifications in industrial relations functions in modern concerns. Whether or not the North American style of 'human resourcing' will ever replace the conventional duties of the personnel or labour specialist is open to doubt, but whatever the nomenclature here, an expanding industrial relations function in the establishment could well be accompanied by qualitative changes in the role itself. In favourable economic circumstances this could encourage not only so-called 'self-actualisation' programmes but also the notion of resourceful humans capable of resolving a range of multi-dimensional roles and functions in both work and leisure spheres. But in the conditions of economic uncertainty and high unemployment which seem likely, in practice management would still have to be the prime agency for the introduction of imaginative work sharing and other programmes which would involve complex moves of personnel in and out of paid employment. Again, with the major technical and other changes which seem to be certain in manufacturing industry, the role of personnel and industrial relations officers would appear likely to become increasingly influential in the enterprise.

It could be anticipated, however, that managerial strategies in industrial relations will focus more on individual employees and less on the shop stewards and other union representatives than was the case in the 1970s. As we have seen, this is consistent with general managerial attitudes and especially with current hostility to trade union power in Britain at a general level. This state of affairs could well imply that the change towards single-employer *collective* bargaining, the provision of facilities for shop stewards and the involvement of the domestic union organisation in strong bargaining relationships may no longer be so characteristic of the 1980s and the early 1990s. Indeed, in the emergent service and other industries outside manufacturing and the public sector, management could well pursue very different industrial relations and personnel styles involving advanced human resourcing and leadership patterns and the implementation of a series of 'behavioural science' research findings on motivations and involvement in work. Moreover, given a considerable amount of choice of different strategies and objectives and the varied initiatives of managers in the main employment sectors, it could well be that by the 1990s a range of diverse management roles and policies in industrial relations will be in evidence.

Developments in the trade unions

As far as trade unions are concerned, in recent years an impressive array of British industrial relations scholarship has developed on various aspects of these important organisations (see e.g. Bain and Elsheikh, 1976; Bain and Price, 1980; Brown, 1981; Undy et al., 1981). This has the further consequence that predictions about the future are rather less hazardous than in some other areas of labour-management relations. Our detailed analysis of trade unions will begin by an assessment of the factors affecting changes in these bodies. This will be followed by a review of dominant trends in trade unions and by an outline of prospects for the future based on these relatively secure foundations.

The conditions of change in trade unions have been the subject of several detailed studies but 'Change in Trade Unions' (Undy et al., 1981) is the most recent. In this comprehensive account of forces which have helped to shape trade unions in modern Britain, the processes of change have been classified into factors which are *external* to a given union and those which are rooted in *internal* developments. Moreover, the external factors were further divided into the economic environment, management and employer attitudes and policies, government attitudes and policies, and attitudes and policies of other unions and the Trades Union Congress. In the first place, then, the economic environment was seen to be characterised by declining employment opportunities, rising inflation and low levels of economic growth. This milieu, too, was seen to be conducive to a rise in militancy and to a breakdown in parochialism that helped to push unions such as the National Union of Teachers and the National and Local Government Officers' Association into the TUC. The influence of employer and management attitudes and policy was particularly manifested in changes in the bargaining relationship. In particular, in manufacturing industry, managements took the lead in 'sponsoring moves away from national bargaining during the late 1960's and early 1970's' (Undy et al., 1981: 319). Meanwhile, government policy could be detected in initiatives in three rather different areas: incomes policy, general legislation affecting trade unions and 'the consequences of the 1964 Act which eased the legal requirements for union mergers' (Undy et al., 1981: 320). And finally, the attitudes and policies of other unions and the TUC appeared to have determined the shape and direction of the merger movements which have intensified in recent years.

Nevertheless, in 'Change in Trade Unions', considerable attention was also focused on the role of internal factors. These were broadly divided into two groups: 'those that relate to the attitudes and policies of particular union groups, and those that concern the influence of particular decision-making structures' (Undy et al., 1981: 324). To begin with, then, as far as the mass membership and the minority of lay activists were concerned, rank-and-file pressure led to significant changes in the bargaining strategy of several unions in the 1960s and 1970s. However, in the view of Undy et al., national leaders have been by far the most significant group affecting internal changes in trade unions. Indeed, they would appear to have had a dominant influence over mergers, internal union government (especially the carrying through of formal change and administrative innovation) and on job regulation. More generally, too, as Undy et al. observed (1981: 326-7):

> All in all, it seems to us that one of the central conclusions to emerge from this study is that, so far as change is concerned, a very great deal depends on the attitudes, objectives and calibre of general secretaries or their equivalents. A union that is led by a conservative or lazy general secretary, who is content to accept the traditional view of the organization's scope, aims and structure, will launch few initiatives designed to achieve conscious and deliberate change. Yet desire to innovate and influence events, and even an abundance of energy, will not usually be sufficient to overcome the forces of inertia, prejudice or interest. There also has to be above-average political skill, and not a little courage.

Lastly, however, the decision-making structure of the union was also viewed as a relevant factor in the internal processes of change within trade unions. Thus, as Undy et al. noted, receptiveness to change was higher where the rules provided that decisions were centralised and concentrated, where the powers given to the national leadership under the rules could be exercised with flexibility and discretion, where existing rules could be changed and adapted to fit new circumstances and where the existence and strength of organised factions were both limited.

These factors, then, provide a comprehensive guide to the most significant forces affecting processes of change within trade unions. But what, it may be reasonably asked, have been the dominant developments in recent years within the labour movement and what are the prospects of these continuing to be prominent components of the patterns of change in trade unions in the 1980s? In order to attempt to shed light on these central questions, the analysis continues by way of an examination of the following evolutionary changes within trade unions and in their relationship with management.

(1) An overall increase in trade union density, a decline in the number of unions, the concentration of membership in the larger associations and substantial merger activity.

(2) The growth in white collar and managerial unionism, in trade unionism amongst women and in public sector trade unionism.

(3) The rise of shop stewards and plant-level collective bargaining activities in general, the growth in the number of full-time shop stewards and in the closed shop.

(4) The dominant position of single-employer agreements covering one or more factories within a company.

(5) Changes in internal government of unions, the use of postal ballots and lay activists becoming more significant in the decision-making processes within trade unions.

(6) Transformations in the economic, political and social aspirations of rank-and-file members.

In the first place, therefore, the 1970s witnessed a substantial increase in the overall number of trade unionists in Britain (see Table 2.1) and a corresponding expansion in union density (i.e. the proportion of the employed workforce in trade unions). Indeed, trade union membership rose nationally from 43 per cent of the workforce in 1968 to 54 per cent in 1978 (Brown, 1981: 120). Moreover, as we have seen, such a development has been widely attributed to inflation, to government intervention in labour relations and to a steady increase in the concentration of ownership in British industry (Price and Bain, 1976; Brown, 1981: 120-1). Historically, too, as may be seen again from Table 2.1, there has been a tendency for the number of trade unions to decline; a situation brought about partly by merger activity and partly by the increasing concentration of union membership in larger associations. For example, in 1955, 65 per cent of union members were in the top twelve associations, a figure which reached 71 per cent in 1978 (MacBeath, 1979: 6).

The concentration of trade union membership in the largest associations is a product partly of internal factors (notably the policy of strategically placed trade union officials) but, above

Table 2.1 *Major changes in the constituent trade unions of the Trades Union Congress*

		No. of unions				No. of delegates			
		1965	1970	1975	1980	1965	1970	1975	1980
1	Mining and quarrying	3	3	2	3	101	65	56	59
2	Railways	3	3	3	3	41	40	40	42
3	Transport (other than railways)	10	9	6	6	93	97	93	109
4	Shipbuilding	3	3	1	1	20	13	12	12
5	Engineering, founding and vehicle building	19	13	10	10	113	96	80	80
6	Technical, engineering and scientific	–	5	5	3	–	38	48	61
7	Electricity	3	1	1	1	31	34	30	35
8	Iron and steel and minor metal trade	15	12	10	9	48	35	34	30
9	Building, woodworking and furnishing	16	9	5	3	69	58	48	42
10	Printing and paper	9	6	6	5	59	64	47	80
11	Textiles	28	25	17	13	48	44	37	26
12	Clothing, leather and boot and shoe	12	10	6	6	46	51	39	43
13	Glass, pottery, chemicals, food, drink, tobacco, brush making and distribution	14	11	9	9	67	67	63	69
14	Agriculture	1	1	1	1	16	19	17	12
15	Public employees	8	11	9	12	70	126	171	215
16	Civil servants	9	14	10	13	72	97	111	147
17	Professional, clerical and entertainment	15	12	9	10	61	54	42	68
18	General workers	4	2	1	1	58	62	64	73
		172	150	111	109	1,013	1,060	1,030	1,203

		Membership			
		1965	1970	1975	1980
1	Mining and quarrying	513,007	321,940	276,636	289,448
2	Railways	386,786	290,111	272,762	277,051
3	Transport (other than railways)	1,547,986	1,656,704	1,966,303	2,203,515
4	Shipbuilding	120,309	124,153	129,598	129,712
5	Engineering, founding and vehicle building	1,387,561	1,465,691	1,449,511	1,449,800
6	Technical, engineering and scientific	-	242,640	523,242	745,063
7	Electricity	334,385	392,401	444,189	420,000
8	Iron and steel and minor metal trades	217,951	151,786	144,473	137,998
9	Building, woodworking and furnishing	525,363	380,536	346,830	435,493
10	Printing and paper	364,293	391,765	306,582	429,257
11	Textiles	180,729	148,470	130,092	111,886
12	Clothing, leather and boot and shoe	262,934	260,662	262,553	259,561
13	Glass, pottery, chemicals, food, drink, tobacco, brush making and distribution	475,246	455,532	495,506	606,108
14	Agriculture	135,000	115,000	90,000	85,000
15	Public employees	695,829	1,200,740	1,615,452	2,235,985
16	Civil servants	520,842	657,808	785,696	959,116
17	Professional, clerical and entertainment	311,571	338,278	272,489	430,452
18	General workers	791,220	807,853	883,810	967,153
		8,771,012	9,402,170	10,363,724	12,172,508

Source: TUC Annual Reports

all, reflects the ability of 'open unions' to 'spread the risks' across a series of occupations and sectors and hence to avoid losses of membership occasioned by technical and economic change. By contrast, closed craft unions are highly dependent upon the possession of particular skills which modern technologies have tended inexorably to undermine. Similarly, those trade unions which are confined to a single industry (such as mining or railways) are clearly vulnerable to long-term changes in employment in their particular sectors of the economy. Hence, the National Union of Mineworkers had the largest body of members in the TUC until the 1930s but had fallen to tenth position in 1980. Again, the National Union of Railwaymen was in fifth position in 1955 but had declined to seventeenth place in 1980. Such movements are set out in Table 2.2 which shows the changes in trade union membership in the twenty largest trade unions in Great Britain in five-year periods from 1965 to 1980. It should be mentioned, too, that there are certain industries (notably construction, printing, shipbuilding, textiles and clothing) where a decline in union membership and employment has only been masked by union mergers (MacBeath, 1979: 2).

The most interesting developments in Britain's trade unions in recent years have been associated, however, with the substantial increase in white-collar and managerial trade unionism, in the propensity of women to join trade unions in increasing numbers and in the spectacular growth of public sector trade unionism. To some extent each departure has its origins in a closely connected group of causative influences stemming from government involvement in the economy and in industrial relations, the recognition policies of management that have tended to produce substantial differences in union density in the public and private sectors respectively, the changing pattern of occupations in the wider society, and a greater willingness of white-collar, managerial and female employees to join trade unions associated with corresponding attitudinal changes in periods of high inflation.

Taking first, then, the growth of white-collar and managerial unionism, by the 1970s, one-third of all trade unionists were white-collar workers and, as Price and Bain have documented (1976: 345)

> Between 1964 and 1970 total white-collar union membership increased by 33.8 per cent, an increase over a six-year period which was greater than that recorded in the previous sixteen years; and in the four years to the end of 1974, a further 671,000 members were added.... By 1974, 36 per cent of all union members were white-collar employees compared with 26 per cent ten years earlier, and with 21 per cent in 1948.

Table 2.2 *Changes in trade union membership in the twenty largest trade unions in Great Britain*

	Union	Membership 1965	1970	1975	1980	% change 1975/1980
1	Transport and General Workers' Union (TGWU)	1,443,738	1,531,607	1,856,165	2,086,281	+12.4
2	Amalgamated Union of Engineering Workers (AUEW) (E, C, F sections)	1,081,726	1,195,710	1,300,477	1,378,580	+11.1
3	General and Municipal Workers' Union (GMWU)	795,767	803,653	881,356	967,153	+ 9.7
4	National and Local Government Officers' Association (NALGO)	348,528	397,069	625,163	753,226	+20.5
5	National Union of Public Employees (NUPE)	248,041	305,222	584,485	691,770	+18.4
6	Association of Scientific, Technical and Managerial Staffs (ASTMS)	65,114	123,800	374,000	491,000	+31.3
7	Union of Shop, Distributive and Allied Workers (USDAW)	349,230	316,387	327,302	470,017	+43.6
8	Electrical, Electronic Telecommunication and Plumbing Union (EEPTU)	282,741	392,401	420,000	420,000	0.0
9	Union of Construction, Allied Trades and Technicians (UCATT)	347,352	227,287	278,127	347,777	+25.0
10	National Union of Mineworkers (NUM)	446,453	297,108	261,871	253,142	- 3.4
11	National Union of Teachers (NUT)	263,000	290,440	281,855	248,896	-13.2

Table 2.2 *Changes in trade union membership in the twenty largest trade unions in Great Britain*

Union	Membership				% change
	1965	1970	1975	1980	1975/1980
12 Civil and Public Services Association (CPSA)	145,775	181,133	224,742	223,884	- 0.4
13 Confederation of Health Service Employees (COHSE)	67,588	77,808	167,200	212,930	+27.4
14 Society of Graphical and Allied Trades (SOGAT)	225,046	235,927	195,522	205,784	+ 5.2
15 Union of Post Office Workers (UPW)/ Union of Communication Workers (UCW)	175,491	198,037	185,000	203,452	+10.0
16 Amalgamated Union of Engineering Workers (TASS) (AUEW)	71,707	86,789	140,784	200,954	+42.7
17 National Union of Railwaymen (NUR)	254,687	191,274	180,429	180,000	÷ 0.2
18 Association of Professional Executive, Clerical and Computer Staff (APEX)	-	-	136,097	151,206	+11.1
19 Amalgamated Society of Boilermakers, Shipwrights, Blacksmiths and Structural Workers (ASBSBSW)	122,981	123,580	136,193	129,712	- 5.0
20 Post Office Engineering Union (POEU)	91,821	111,906	124,682	125,723	+ 0.8

Source: TUC Annual Reports

While the success of unions in the white-collar sector is not disputed there is some argument as to underlying causes. In essence, there is a cleavage between sociological analyses which have focused largely upon fluctuations in the class position and class consciousness of white-collar workers and the opposing industrial relations critique which contends that a limited number of economic and technical changes have been paramount. Both explanations admit subjective factors but while sociologists have tended to concentrate upon modifications in class or status imagery, industrial relations scholars have emphasised the issues of recognition and a desire for job regulation (see Lockwood, 1958; Blackburn, 1967; Prandy, 1965; Bain, 1970; Bain, Coates and Ellis, 1973; Crompton, 1976). Whatever the correct interpretation, the spectacular growth of individual white collar unions is clearly evident from Table 2.2 and, above all, in the case of the National and Local Government Officers' Association which is now Britain's fourth largest trade union. Indeed, the character of the TUC is gradually being transformed by this development.

During the last decade or so, the expansion of white-collar occupations and of white-collar trade unionism has been paralleled by a similar process taking place in managerial unionism. This growth can doubtless be attributed in part to the proliferation of administrative functions, to growing size of enterprise and to recognition policies in the public sector. But in the British Institute of Management survey the three main variables which were found to be especially significant in accounting for managers joining unions were the presence of a union in the employing association (this is coterminous but distinct from recognition), being in the public sector and the commitment to collectivist principles on the part of the managers themselves (Poole et al., 1981). In the case of individual unions, too, such as the Association of Scientific, Technical and Managerial Staffs, part of the explanation for substantial growth has to be sought in terms of merger activity.

Since the Second World War, however, women workers have provided the largest single source of recruitment for trade unions. At present approximately one-quarter of the TUC is composed of women, while in the past two decades almost two-thirds of all new members have been female. Moreover, between 1960 and 1966 a 70 per cent increase in trade unionism amongst women was recorded and, as Price and Bain have noted, taking the period 1948-74, female union membership and density advanced at a greater pace than male membership, with the female proportion increasing from 18 per cent to 27 per cent and the level of union density from 25.7 per cent to 36.7 per cent (Price and Bain, 1976: 347). Recent figures for individual trade unions are set out in Table 2.3, where the very high percentages of female members in the Confederation

Table 2.3 *Numbers and percentages of women in the twenty largest trade unions in Great Britain*

Unions	Membership								% change
	1965	%	1970	%	1975	%	1980	%	1975/80
1 Transport and General Workers' Union (TGWU)	194,064	13.4	213,424	13.9	286,829	15.5	342,769	16.4	+12.0
2 Amalgamated Union of Engineering Workers (AUEW) (E, C, F sections)	92,294	8.5	127,910	10.7	174,323	13.4	167,664	12.2	-10.4
3 General and Municipal Workers' Union (GMWU)	186,098	23.4	219,799	27.4	285,357	32.4	328,234	33.9	+11.5
4 National and Local Government Officers' Association (NALGO)	123,410	35.4	145,800	36.7	218,100	34.9	355,757	43.6	+16.3
5 National Union of Public Employees (NUPE)	117,000	47.2	173,058	56.7	321,302	55.0	461,180	66.7	+14.4
6 Association of Scientific, Technical and Managerial Staffs (ASTMS)	500	0.8	4,000	3.2	62,000	16.6	85,925	17.5	+13.9
7 Union of Shop, Distributive and Allied Workers (USDAW)	166,382	47.6	157,941	49.9	203,952	62.3	290,285	61.8	+14.2
8 Electrical, Electronic Telecommunication and Plumbing Union (EEPTU)	24,194	8.6	40,856	10.4	52,996	12.6	43,000	10.2	-12.3

9	Union of Construction Allied Trades and Technicians (UCATT)	–	–	–	–	1,881	0.7	1,762	0.5	-10.7
10	National Union of Mineworkers (NUM)	–	–	–	–	–	–	–	–	–
11	National Union of Teachers (NUT)	–	–	212,208	80.7	197,453	70.1	156,896	63.0	-12.6
12	Civil and Public Services Association (CPSA)	85,871	58.9	116,551	64.4	145,693	64.8	159,994	71.5	+11.0
13	Confederation of Health Service Employees (COHSE)	33,532	49.6	46,346	59.6	101,059	60.4	164,494	77.2	+16.3
14	Society of Graphical and Allied Trades (SOGAT)	–	–	80,378	34.1	69,928	35.8	69,533	33.8	- 1.0
15	Union of Post Office Workers (UPW)/Union of Communication Workers (UCW)	44,779	25.5	49,531	25.0	42,321	22.9	50,863	25.0	+12.0
16	Amalgamated Union of Engineering Workers (TASS)	2,833	4.0	2,646	3.1	9,685	6.9	30,203	15.0	+31.2
17	National Union of Railwaymen (NUM)	7,767	3.0	7,709	4.0	6,611	3.7	9,503	5.3	+14.4
18	Association of Professional, Executive, Clerical and Computer Staff (APEX)	–	–	–	–	75,278	55.3	15,129	56.3	+11.3

Unions	Membership								% change
	1965	%	1970	%	1975	%	1980	%	1975/80
19 Amalgamated Society of Boilermakers, Shipwrights, Blacksmiths and Structural Workers (ASBSBSW)	110	0.09	-	-	156	0.11	231	0.18	+14.8
20 Post Office Engineering Union (POEU)	750	0.8	1,770	1.6	3,957	3.2	3,522	2.8	+11.2

Source: TUC Annual Reports.

of Health Service Employees, the Civil and Public Services Association, the National Union of Public Employees, the National Union of Teachers and the Union of Shop, Distributive and Allied Workers are particularly worthy of mention.

Nevertheless, as Lewenhak (1977) has recognised, trade unionism amongst women is no new phenomenon but can be traced back through many centuries. Similarly, the textile industry in particular has always provided a major occupational base for the enhancement of female unionism. But, except in wartime, female employment was restrained until relatively recently. However, the influx of married women seeking paid work, coupled with a major shift in occupations and the extension of white-collar opportunities, have all proved important spurs for an expansion of unionism amongst women. Moreover, the changing attitudes of women to work and careers would seem to be a durable phenomenon in British society that is likely, in turn, to have considerable repercussions for trade unionism in the future.

The particular association between trade unionism and the public sector should also be emphasised, since, in the years ahead, the relative prospects for employment in private and nationalised concerns respectively are bound to have substantial effect upon trade union growth as a whole. This applies especially to white-collar and managerial unionism but such developments will also have far-reaching implications for those trade unions which recruit solely in the public sector and which experienced very rapid rises in membership in the 1970s (such as COHSE, CPSA and NUPE).

The expansion of the shop steward system has also been of fundamental importance as far as recent changes in trade unionism are concerned. Such a development has deep historical roots (Clegg, 1979; Hinton, 1973), but it has been particularly characteristic of the period from the 1950s onwards when full employment, greater technical complexity and enterprise size on the one hand and the breakdown of the wartime consensus on the other began to have a significant impact on the shape of Britain's trade unions. Shop stewards are of course plant-based union representatives and in the recent Warwick survey it was found that they exist for manual workers in about 73 per cent of establishments and for non-manual employees in approximately 34 per cent of cases (Brown, 1981: 62). Again, the post of senior representative or convenor was found in 74 per cent of establishments where there were manual shop stewards and in 61 per cent where there were non-manual shop stewards. Moreover, the number of full-time shop stewards probably quadrupled in the 1970s (Brown, 1981: 120) associated with the attempts by managers to develop some formal collective bargaining procedures in the plant (Brown et al., 1978). Workforce size has been acknowledged to be very important in accounting for variations in recognition of senior stewards, in the presence of senior stewards in the plant, in the occurrence of regular steward meetings, and in combine committee meetings (Brown, 1981: 62-7).

The growth of shop steward organisations at factory level has also been a barometer of the changing patterns of influence over decisions within the plant. Hence, in a series of studies, the impact of shop stewards over such issues as labour mobility, the manning of machinery, job demarcation, work study, 'dilutee' labour, union demarcation, working conditions, wages, hours, holidays, discipline and employment issues has been charted (McCarthy and Parker, 1968; Evans, 1973; Batstone et al., 1977). Indeed, in a careful study of shop steward influence, Batstone et al. (1977: 261) observed that

> In brief, the power of the domestic organization meant that management had little freedom in introducing any form of change in production which might have an adverse impact upon workers. Major changes in production methods involved possibly lengthy negotiations over effort and reward. The same was true of shorter-term changes. If management required temporary variations or exceptional patterns of work, they were generally bound either by negotiation or by a network of rules which were the product of past negotiations.

To be sure, this is not to imply that all shop stewards are militant. Indeed, a series of studies have revealed a number of shop steward types in which varying commitments to trade union principles and leadership roles may be discerned (Pedler, 1973/4; Poole, 1974; Batstone et al., 1977). Moreover, although with the onset of the depression in the economy some of the influence of shop stewards will perforce have been diminished, this in no way reduces the impact of this momentous change in the nature of Britain's trade unions in this respect in the last quarter of a century.

The rise of the shop steward has also been to some extent associated with the continuing importance of the closed shop in British industry. An early study by McCarthy (1964) pointed out that, in manufacturing industry, approximately 25 per cent of employers were covered by closed shop agreements. In recent investigations, however, Gennard, Dunn and Wright (1980) suggested a minimum coverage of the closed shop in manufacturing of 39 per cent, while Brown (1981) found that, on the basis of returns from employers, a figure of 31 per cent would seem to be indicated. However, this percentage was reached after assuming that the closed shop is 'all but insignificant' in establishments in which fewer than fifty workers are employed. But if this is not the case (and there are grounds for a rather different premise) a figure nearer that of Gennard et al. may well be the most accurate. But, its character has undoubtedly depended greatly on recognition by management. Indeed, as Brown (1981: 59) has recently observed:

> There can be little doubt that the character of the closed shop is changing. The spread of union membership agreements, especially in industries where there has been little previous experience of the closed shop, is involving management in its administration with a degree of formality that would often have been unthinkable only a decade ago. Furthermore, our survey suggested a clear tendency for more recently concluded closed shops to be more single-union than they were in the past. The closed shop as a reflection of workplace solidarity may be increasingly being replaced by an institution which is seen by management and the wider union primarily as an instrument of procedural discipline.

At all events, the last decade has almost certainly witnessed a change in the pattern of collective bargaining of momentous significance for Britain's overall system of industrial relations. This has ostensibly been manifested in the transformation of a framework which was once dominated by multi-employer agreements and its replacement by single-employer agreements covering one or more factories within a company (Brown, 1981: 118). Indeed, according to the recent Warwick report, multi-employer agreements now cover only a quarter of the manual and a tenth of the non-manual workforce in manufacturing establishments (Brown, 1981: 118). However, there are important grounds for caution in the interpretation of these data since the survey was carried out at the time of an incomes policy and the relaxation of rigid pay norms is generally acknowledged to encourage more multi-level agreements. Again, the smallest firms (where multi-employer agreements are particularly prevalent) were excluded and, when more than one level of negotiation was mentioned by respondents, for analytical purposes, only the most important in terms of the pay award was selected. By the same token, too, foreign enterprises (rather than indigenous companies) were found to be particularly likely to avoid multi-employer agreements, the continued membership of employers' associations suggests that such agreements have not been abandoned wholesale and the growth of the public sector has naturally encouraged single-employer agreements which are typically reached at a relatively high *level* of negotiation involving full-time trade union officers.

This overall trend to single-employer agreements, though, has been highly significant for trade unions since it has on balance reinforced the pivotal position of shop stewards in the processes of wage determination and in the union experiences of rank-and-file members. Moreover, in conjunction with the various conditions which helped to sustain the growth in the shop steward system, this development has been clearly associated with an increasing managerial professionalism in the labour relations field and, especially, with the expansion in the role of personnel and industrial relations officer in the administrative structure of management itself (cf. Brown, 1981: 118-19).

Turning, then, more specifically to trade union government, the shift in the locus of power within unions to plant level has had significant implications for discussions on trade union democracy and administration. This is not to suggest that such issues as participation rates in trade union branches outside the enterprise, the characteristics of the activists in the union (cf. Fosh, 1981) and the formation of factions and so on are not important. But it is to imply that the study of workplace-based branches and of the involvement of members in shop steward elections and in decisions on, say, whether or not to take industrial action in the plant have become increasingly fundamental concerns. Moreover, as Batstone et al. have observed, 'in the debate on trade union government, the terms democracy and oligarchy tend to be used not merely to refer to the distribution of power but also the purposes to which that power is used' (1977: 270). Thus, on these assumptions, the attitudes and beliefs of the 'quasi-elite' of shop stewards in particular have also clearly become central issues in the evolving discussions on the nature and character of trade union democracy.

This is also an important consideration in the case of the various proposals which have been formulated to facilitate the use of secret ballots in elections of officials, in the calling and ending of strikes and in decisions on the revision of trade union rules. After all, in most cases the crucial locus of union power in the modern era remains largely unaffected by such legislation. Hence, to be effective, postal ballots would almost certainly have to be mandatory and a lengthy and deep economic depression would be necessary to weaken plant-based union structures and to bring about a further transformation of union power back to the wider national, regional and district hierarchies.

No sociological account of trade unionism and its likely development in the future would be complete, however, without some reference to the attitudes of rank-and-file members and to their willingness to seek radical or conservative solutions to their particular concerns in the years ahead. Moreover, in industrial sociological writings there have of course been a series of studies of the attitudes and behaviour of workers at enterprise level (see e.g. Goldthorpe et al., 1968; Beynon and Blackburn, 1972; Beynon, 1973; Gallie, 1978; Blackburn and Mann, 1979). In order to set out trade unionists' attitudes in a systematic form, however, an approach based on Weberian (1968) categories of social action is clearly valuable (cf. Poole, 1981).

Table 2.4 *Union members' perceptions and the categories of social action*

General categories of social action	Perceptions of trade unionism
1 Instrumentally rational, that is, determined by expectations as to the behaviour of objects in the environment and of other human beings; these expectations are used as 'conditions' or 'means' for the attainment of the actor's own rationally pursued and calculated ends	1 Instrumentally rational orientation to a variety of union objectives such as safety and welfare, wages and working conditions, job regulation and the democractic government of industry
2 Value rational, that is, determined by a conscious belief in the value for its own sake of some ethical, aesthetic, religious or other form of behaviour, independently of its prospects of success	2 Value rational orientation to the principle of trade unionism as an end in itself and even to the advancement of workers' rights through socialist, political and economic action
3 Affectual (especially emotional), that is, determined by the actor's specific affects or feeling states	3 Affectual orientation to the community and solidarity of union and workgroup
4 Traditional, that is, determined by ingrained habituation	4 Traditional orientation to union activities and to the habituation of 'custom and practice' in the workplace itself

As far as rank-and-file attitudes to trade unions are concerned, although even amongst significant numbers of trade union members themselves there may well be mounting opposition to union power and to the tactics pursued by particular unions, expectations concerning union objectives still appear to have risen in the last decade or so. Thus despite the fact that affectual or emotional commitments to unionism have probably declined in the post-war period, during the 1970s the demands of rank-and-file members embraced not only a series of specific objectives (such as on wages, working conditions, health and safety and participation in management), but also principles of social justice coupled with the determination to maintain a series of traditional customs and practices at workplace level.

To discuss the future of trade unionism in a realistic way thus involves drawing out a series of inferences from the developments in the external and internal factors which affect changes in trade unions and from a review of some of the dominant trends which, as we have seen, have been evident in trade unions in recent years. Taking first of all, then, trade union growth, there is little doubt that union recruitment will be taking place in a milieu far more hostile to trade unionism than has been the case from the late 1960s up until 1980. Indeed, as Undy et al. (1981) have pointed out, demographic developments are likely to increase the size of the potential labour force by about 2 million by the end of the 1980s. Moreover, manufacturing industry can be expected to decline as a source of employment (if only because of technological change rather than unplanned, de-industrialisation) and there may well be considerable opposition to a further major expansion in public sector services. Again, trends of this nature would be reinforced by further unemployment which will not only perforce result in a decline in total union membership but which will also tend to be accompanied by increased managerial hostility to union recognition.

Nevertheless, the very magnitude of the problems in the external union environment may well be conducive to substantial merger activities and to the loss of many smaller unions as the largest associations become increasingly dominant. We have already argued that craft unions are particularly vulnerable to new technological developments, while the massive job losses in substantial parts of the manufacturing sector are likely to stimulate fresh mergers amongst single industry unions. Similarly, an adverse external milieu may well be a spur to a number of white-collar unions to amalgamate with similarly placed organisations. Hence, even if overall union density were to decline in the next decade (and in the light of recent trends in membership this is very likely), such a development could well be accompanied by a marked tendency to further concentration of membership in the largest associations.

Changes in the pattern of occupations, however, will be favourable to the development of white-collar unionism in the forthcoming decade. Employment is thus likely to expand in managerial, professional and technical occupations. Again, the growth of the services sector may well be conducive to the relative advance of women in employment vis-a-vis men. Hence, although white-collar unionism will probably not expand at the rate of the previous decade, and the particularly advantageous recruitment circumstances in the public sector may not be repeated in the 1980s, the significance of non-manual unionism and of unionism amongst women for Britain's labour movement is almost certain to continue.

Turning, then, to the shop steward system and to the dominance of single employer agreements in union-management negotiations, future prediction is made difficult by the uncertainties which surround the state of overall economic activity in the next decade and by the vagaries of managerial strategy in these areas. It should be emphasised, though, that economic buoyancy and favourable managerial policies (such as the provision of shop steward facilities and the willingness to to negotiate with lay activists) have been the mainstay for the rise of shop stewards (and particularly full-time shop stewards) and of agreements confined to a single company. Indeed, on one view, the current structure of workplace-based unionism is vulnerable to the exigencies of the economic climate in the 1980s. Hence, as Brown (1981: 120) has pointed out:

> Despite those apparent improvements in their security, trade unions face fresh causes for concern. Where shop steward organizations have sprung up in factories with little tradition of workplace bargaining, they may owe the superficial sophistication of their facilities and procedures more to the administrative needs of management than to the bargaining achievements of the workforce.

Thus, even though the structure of single-employer agreements is unlikely to be wholly transformed since it is so clearly suited to a professional management operating on an organisational logic, in many enterprises, managerial and administrative personnel may attempt to deal directly with the workforce and hence to bypass the plant-based unions entirely.

With respect to union government, the role of wider political and legislative agencies has already been the subject of detailed comment and any further review would be superfluous at this point. Nevertheless, it is worth mentioning that a number of internal factors may well impinge on the process of union democracy and administration in the decade ahead. Indeed, as Undy et al. have observed, the trends towards decentralisation and diffusion within unions are likely to continue. After all, the number of full-time shop stewards is now considerably higher than the number of full-time officials and this tends to produce divisions between the general secretary and the executive (Undy et al., 1981: 336-7). Moreover, although energetic and politically astute full-time officers may well be able to exert a substantial influence over the development of their associations, the growth of factionalism in British unions in the future remains a strong probability.

Finally, on present trends, it seems likely that a considerable measure of industrial conflict and union militancy will remain characteristic of Britain's overall pattern of industrial relations in the period in question. Economic conditions may well reduce the incidence of strikes in certain employment sectors, government legislation may have a marginal impact in this context and continuing inflation could ensure that wage issues are the focus of hostility in bargaining encounters. But the fragmented structure of British unions coupled with the appreciable rise in rank-and-file expectations since the Second World War are unlikely to signal other than substantial industrial unrest. To be sure, there are other possible options which we shall examine in the final section but without a transformation of social values and more cohesive structures of trade unionism and the machinery for collective bargaining it is difficult to foresee any other outcome.

Legislation on industrial relations

During the course of the twentieth century, the involvement of the legislature in industrial relations has expanded to become a phenomenon of considerable moment in British political life. Naturally, the objectives enshrined in the different types of legislation have varied but, as we have seen, a common element has been that the main political parties have increasingly sought legislative means to facilitate changes in labour relations at both national and local levels. Indeed, an indication of these developments may be provided by a mention of some of the principal enactments and forays which, in the past fifteen or so years, have been designed ostensibly to reshape the employment relationship:

The Contracts of Employment Act, 1963
The Trade Union Amalgamation Act, 1964
The Redundancy Payments Act, 1965
The Race Relations Acts, 1965, 1968, 1976
The Equal Pay Act, 1970
The Industrial Relations Act, 1971
The Trade Union and Labour Relations Act, 1974
The Health and Safety at Work Act, 1974
The Sex Discrimination Act, 1975

The Industry Act, 1975
The Employment Protection Act, 1975
The Trade Union and Labour Relations (Amendment) Act, 1976
The Bullock Report, 1977
The White Paper on Industrial Democracy, 1978
The Employment Act, 1980
The Employment Act, 1982

We have already dealt at length with the general trend towards 'corporatism' which has provided a basis for the analysis of these departures and thus any further review would be superfluous at this juncture. Nevertheless, while the specific types of legislation which will eventuate in the next ten years are by no means easy to predict and again cannot reasonably be discussed without reference to wider political developments, there are five areas in which further legal action would be expected:

(1) Industrial democracy and employee participation;

(2) The reinforcement of legislation on the rights of minority groups and women in employment;

(3) Facilitative legislation encouraging various worksharing and flexible working arrangements;

(4) Restrictions on various types of trade union behaviour;

(5) European initiatives providing support for changes in these and other contexts.

In each of these areas we shall examine, in Section 3 (Policy Implications), the more specific developments which would seem probable in these highly significant aspects of labour relations, but a brief outline of probable legislation emanating from Europe would be valuable at this point. Indeed, on the assumption of the United Kingdom remaining a member of the EEC, European legislation is likely to have an increasingly marked influence on Britain's overall system of industrial relations. Indeed, there are at present a series of measures at various stages in the 'community's legislative pipeline' some of which have already been approved by the Council of Ministers. Hence, in so far as the interests of workers are concerned, Peel has listed the following measures, all of which are likely to have some effect upon Britain's industrial relations in the next decade (Peel, 1979: 88).

Security of employment
Directive on collective redundancies
Directive on acquired rights of workers
Directive on national laws relating to mergers
Directive on insolvency procedures

Conditions of employment

Joint committees (eight in existence, many more in prospect)
Proposed regulation on statute for European companies
Proposed fifth directive on company structure, including employee participation
Harmonisation of labour law, giving participation in works councils of parent company for employees of group subsidiaries
Suitable representation of the interests of employees of public limited liability companies
Measures to limit overtime

These, then, are some of the changes in industrial relations legislation which may well feature prominently in Britain in the next ten years. The details on legislative proposals thus bring to a close the second principal section of the report, in which employers' associations and management on the one hand and the trade unions on the other have also been examined in considerable detail.

Policy implications

In the final section of this report on the patterns of British industrial relations up to the early 1990s attention will focus on a number of areas where initiatives are likely in the period in question. These include: industrial democracy and employee participation, worksharing and flexible work roles and relationships, quality of working life programmes, European initiatives, trade union legislation, managerial 'human resourcing' strategies, the position of women and minority ethnic groups in the employment relationship, incomes policy and industrial conflict. The analysis is then concluded by a consideration of the problems of an excessive reliance on collective bargaining and by an outline of a general strategy which may begin to affect industrial relations over the next decade.

Industrial democracy and employee participation

The emergence of a comprehensive framework of legislation on industrial democracy and employee participation is widely acknowledged to be long overdue in Britain. Such a development cannot be predicted with certainty since, historically, interest in schemes of this type has tended to be greatest in periods of full employment with substantial labour unrest. Hence, the magnitude of the economic problems in the 1980s may conceivably deflect attention away from comprehensive legislative reforms in this area. Yet to be effective, in any future policy there must be an attempt to involve the ordinary worker and to develop machinery in an integrated way at a number of different levels (shop, department, enterprise and company). The conclusions of the Industrial Democracy in Europe study are thus worth quoting in this respect (IDE, 1981: 342):

> Any strategy for democratisation - whether it is the management's, the union's or a joint strategy - aiming at equalisation of power has to include systematic development along several dimensions - rules for participation, the development of a democratic leadership style, and information activities. Strategically, it seems that extending the formal regulations for participation, particularly in medium-range personnel matters creates involvement and rising expectations leading to a self-reinforcing cycle.... We assume that once the basic rights of employees (security and the right to participate) have been legally established and guaranteed, the need emerges for a more democratic approach to the solutions and problems associated with providing industrial democracy.

More specifically, too, on the basis of research evidence, the following points in a general policy seem to be especially crucial (cf. IDE, 1981):

(1) Legislation to provide a basic framework of rights and obligations. This could be facilitative and open in the first instance in so far as institutional structure is concerned but it would seem to be the most important single basis for effective influence and involvement on the part of employees.

(2) An emphasis on democratic leadership styles which appear to be of substantial relevance in any given socio-economic and political context. The encouragement of more women to become managers could help in this respect.

(3) The nurturing of an effective power base for employees. This is perhaps typically and most appropriately advanced through trade unions.

(4) The cardinal importance of developing new socio-technical systems and changing the technology of the plant alongside formal institutional changes. After all, the job level is the most important area for enhancing the influence and involvement of shop-floor employees (rather than representatives) and no worthwhile programme for employee participation should in the future ignore this level of operation.

(5) The development of modes of work organisation with novel conceptions of administrative hierarchies (as they are currently understood) would constitute a worthwhile trend for imaginative insights and research endeavour.

Worksharing

Worksharing is another area in which major industrial relations initiatives are likely in the decade ahead. The types of schemes involved here are multifarious but embrace such measures as the shorter working week, longer holidays, earlier retirement, sabbaticals and job sharing (Gronseth, 1978; Blyton and Hill, 1981; Institute of Manpower Studies, 1981). The assumption that developments will take place along these lines is particularly based on the premise that unemployment will not be reduced by conventional measures, if only because the micro-electronic and other technological revolutions are bound to have dramatic effects upon employment levels in manufacturing industry during the period under review.

It is unlikely, however, that the full benefits of such a policy will be achieved without a comprehensive programme of support based on agreements between all the main industrial relations parties. For this reason, the role of government as a catalyst will continue to be central. But given the massive financial costs of current unemployment benefits, in the long term there could be major economic advantages from the widespread introduction of schemes of this type. Nevertheless, general changes in employment law may well be necessary to persuade employers to introduce such schemes on other than a piecemeal basis. A modification in trade union attitudes to focus on the more imaginative possibilities here rather than on the perennial calls for earlier retirement and the shorter working week would also help to facilitate the introduction of worthwhile ventures. Flexible work roles and relationships, too, might well be popular throughout the working population not least because they promote more balanced patterns of work and leisure by partners in the domestic sphere.

Quality of working life programmes

Interest in integrated and comprehensive approaches to industrial relations reform could further result in a variety of quality of working life programmes, particularly if these proved to be conducive to productivity as well as employee satisfaction. To be sure, in a context of high unemployment there may be rather less pressure in these directions than in the late 1960s and 1970s, but such changes are still entirely consistent with internationally based advanced labour practices (cf. Davis and Cherns, 1975a, 1975b). Moreover, as Walton (1975) has observed, a strategy of this type could encompass the notions of adequate and fair compensation for work, safe and healthy working conditions, immediate opportunity to use and develop human capacities, opportunities for continued growth and security, social integration in the work organisation, constitutionalism in the work organisation, work and the total life space (i.e. a balanced role of work and leisure) and the social relevance of work to life. Again, Peel (1979: 120) has identified the following guidelines in a comprehensive quality of working life programme: clean and safe working conditions; continuity of employment; the right to organise into trade unions; fair and equitable pay relationships; the provision of employee benefits; personnel systems in which individual workers are considered to be human assets; participation in management; a workplace climate which encourages 'openness, a sense of community, and personal equality'; the right to free speech, privacy and dissent; and a balance between work and life style.

European initiatives

On the assumption that Britain remains a member of the EEC, these are the types of development which the Commission and European Parliament favour and promote (cf. Peel, 1979). But a series of further pressures could emanate from Europe for reform of industrial relations and for shifts in work practices. From the vantage point of being Director of Industrial Relations for the Commission of the European Communities, Peel has thus identified six main ideas from Europe, some of which are being enacted on a selective basis, that could influence Britain's industrial relations in the forthcoming years (1979: 177-9)

(1) The foundation would be a national minimum wage, automatically linked to retail prices (the actual level could be set by the National Economic Development Office).

(2) These arrangements would be legally binding and would form a basis for further reforms in industrial relations.

(3) Good conduct bonuses for those workers who do not strike during the duration of an agreement could be introduced.

(4) A Differentials Commission should be established, preferably with all-party support.

(5) The use of secret ballots should be extended particularly in the case of proposed strike action (in West Germany a 75 per cent vote for strike action is required, the initial call coming from the executive committee of the union concerned).

(6) The British picketing laws could be further changed and amended with 'secondary' picketing being prohibited.

Moreover, European initiatives may well prove to be influential in the employment sphere. Attempts by European governments to combat unemployment thus include job creation, preferential hiring, deferred sackings, temporary job creation, early retirement, more time at school (and in further education), labour mobility and controls on overtime and moonlighting (Peel, 1979: Appendix, Figure 4). Increasingly, too, the trade unions and employers' associations may develop along European lines. After all, the European Trade Union Confederation (ETUC) was established in 1973 and the Union of Industries of the European Community (UNICE) in 1958. Further initiatives in employee shareholding, job enrichment, disclosure of information, industrial democracy and incomes policy are also likely to stem from European institutions (cf. Peel, 1979: 105-50). Indeed, although it is more than a decade since both ventures were first introduced, in the area of industrial democracy, important pressures for reform in Britain are contained in both the Statute for European Companies and in the Draft Fifth Directive relating to the decision-making structure of public companies.

Trade union legislation

In the case of trade union legislation, the framework of policy over the next few years is already clear but whether or not the proposals envisaged remain permanently on the statute book depends greatly upon political developments in the 1980s. Moreover, a realistic and comprehensive programme for trade union reform would almost certainly have to involve a *quid pro quo* in terms of, say, disclosure of information and participative rights. In 1982, however, a series of trade union immunities has been removed (notably for unlawful acts which are not 'in contemplation or furtherance of a trade dispute', and for action which is unlawful for individuals by virtue of the limitations to section B of the 1974 Act made by the Employment Act, 1980, in the area of secondary picketing). Moreover, the same measures are designed to amend the present statutory definition of a trade dispute, to legislate against selective dismissals in a strike, to reinforce the provisions of the 1980 Act on the closed shop and to proceed against union labour-only contracts (Green Paper 'Trade Union Immunities', 1981; 'Financial Times', 1981b). The effectiveness of this legislation, however, remains to be seen and a successful and imaginative policy in this sphere might involve encouragement for a series of positive trade union initiatives and activities (including for example, trade union-sponsored modes of job creation, and training and educational programmes).

Managerial 'human resourcing' strategies

At several points in this report we have drawn attention to the pivotal role of managers in industrial relations. Moreover, as one has sought to argue, not only have the managements of British enterprises been largely responsible for the move to single company bargaining in the 1970s, but also they substantially enhanced the growth of plant-based trade union activities by encouraging the role of full-time shop steward and by providing a series of facilities for the effective functioning of trade unions at this level. However, for various reasons (economic and technical change and the reduced power of unions), it is anticipated that, in the 1980s, management will often prefer to develop more individually based personnel and industrial policies founded on the American concept of 'human resourcing' (or perhaps the notion of employees as resourceful humans capable of devising more complex relationships between work and leisure spheres). Again, accompanying increasing management education, a series of major initiatives could well take place in the personnel area, deriving from examples and models which have been tested on an international scale (e.g. in Japan, Western Europe, the United States and even in Third World countries). Thus, in his review of likely developments in personnel management in Britain during the 1980s, Cowan (1980: 25) has made the forceful point that:

> During the 1980s we shall undoubtedly see a transition in society.... Just as we moved from the medieval society to our present industrial society, so shall we gradually move to the post-industrial society. Technology will have liberated large numbers of people from mindless and menial work in the factory, the office and the home. Recreation and leisure will become increasingly important and will receive more attention. Resourceful humans achieving a greater sense of fulfilment from their total activities will regard 'job satisfaction' as only one of their goals and the human resourcing manager of the post-industrial period will see his job in far wider terms than that perceived by the personnel manager of today. Indeed, the leap forward may be across a gap that is as wide as that between the modern personnel officer and the pre-war labour or welfare officer.

Women and minority ethnic groups

The situation of women and minority ethnic groups both in employment and in the institutions of industrial relations (including, not least, the trade unions themselves) will also be a critical issue over the next decade. In so far as women are concerned, there was a marked increase in the number of females in employment in the 1970s (8.9 million in 1971: 10.3 million in 1980), and some of the pressures arising from changing aspirations, higher levels of education, small family size and the life expectancies of women show no obvious signs of abating in the 1980s. This situation is not only likely to occasion further pressures on the job market but it could also be a principal stimulus for some of the worksharing strategies which are envisaged over the period in question.

But the participation of women in public life, in management and in the trade unions has not been commensurate with such general changes. For instance, Williamson, in his survey of 1970 graduates, found that women had only half the chance of men of reaching managerial status (1981: 1), while in the recent survey of a systematically selected sample of BIM members only 1.7 per cent of respondents were female (Mansfield et al., 1981; Poole et al., 1981). The position of women in trade unions is also unsatisfactory in this respect, since although a number of trade unions (such as COHSE, CPSA and NUPE) have a predominantly female membership, this is not reflected in the proportion of women active in the union (whether as full-time officials or as shop stewards) (Lewenhak, 1977; Mackie and Patullo, 1977). Nevertheless, as Mackie and Patullo (1977: 179) have remarked;

> The growth of women's membership of trade unions in recent years reflects both the movement of women out of the house and the growing awareness of their economic power. The impact of female membership is still largely localised, in individual unions, and if women are to achieve full equality at work, they must use the trade union movement. The *Equal Pay Act*, whatever its weaknesses, has already had an impact on women workers and many unions are beginning to realise this. If women learn this lesson - that they can alter the conditions of their working life - their future in trade unionism could be unlimited.

Following on from the recommendations of the Scarman Report (1981), the position of minority ethnic groups in Britain's industries and services and in the institutions of industrial relations is also of central concern to developments in this area in the 1980s. Two rather different patterns seem most likely to be manifest: an increasing pressure on employers and unions to move to quota systems in the selection of personnel from different racial groups for senior positions; and a growing propensity for minority groups to seek recourse to their own institutions. This latter departure, too, would probably involve the setting up of various independent trade unions and specific bodies in the TUC that parallel, say, the women's conference (cf. Mackie and Patullo, 1977: 169). Again, just as in NUPE, for example, various seats on the general council have been reserved for women, a similar system could well evolve for members of minority ethnic groups in a number of leading British trade unions.

Incomes policy

The question of incomes policy is also fundamental in Britain's evolving system of industrial relations. Nevertheless, as Taylor (1980: 446) has cogently remarked:

> A statutory incomes policy, backed by sanctions and punishments, cannot work for long in a free society. It is only possible where democratic institutions have been destroyed. On the other hand, a state of nature in an economy with next to no growth threatens our liberties. The leviathan is an alternative that few wish to see; yet alarmingly few seem ready to fight against the self-destructive irrationalism of the present pay chaos.

Taylor's own prognosis for the future of incomes policy in the 1980s is rather pessimistic with 'the triumph of the Hobbesian scenario of sectionalist greed and strife as the most probable outcome' and with the unions 'taking the full force of the coming social stress' (Taylor, 1980: 455-7). Yet he offers a rather different potential prospect based on a 'broader approach to wage determination' with a belated opportunity for lay activists and full-time officials to become more involved 'in company decision-making through full disclosure of information, closer union co-operation in manpower planning, investment decisions, fringe benefits' and in 'removing the inequalities between blue- and white-collar workers' (Taylor, 1980: 445-6). Moreover, a series of attempts have been made over the years to develop tripartite national machinery designed to facilitate discussions on overall pay policy and on the differentials between groups. Such arrangements, too, could well emerge with fresh vigour in a changing political milieu in the latter part of the 1980s. In this respect, too, not only could the successful Scandinavian system of tripartite national negotiations (involving government, LO and SAF) be a model, but concerted action by the government, TUC and CBI to plan 'a fairer wage structure within an overall framework of economic reality' (Peel, 1979: 179) could conceivably emerge. Again, 'the synchronisation of settlement dates within a defined period of time each year' is widely considered to be a valuable development (Peel, 1979: 179). Similarly, although the comprehensive introduction of such a policy runs counter to the essentially market strategy of the current government, it may still prove to be attractive in the public sector where such considerations are of lesser import.

Industrial conflict

No analysis of the future of industrial relations in Great Britain would be complete, however, without reference to changing patterns of industrial conflict and, above all, of strike activity. Moreover, in an environment where worker expectations and demands show only limited signs of moderation outside the competitive sectors of the economy, the continued fragmentation of Britain's collective bargaining system and massive technological change are likely to reinforce a high level of union activity and militancy. Indeed, a series of protracted struggles may well take place alongside the trend, which manifested itself in the 1970s, for industrial action which was 'fragmented, partial and diffused in its impact' (Undy et al., 1981: 338). In this latter respect, then, as Undy et al. further observed, 'the conventional "all-out" stoppage, involving a total and indefinite refusal to work', tended to be avoided 'in favour of a locally determined mixture of overtime bans, one-day strikes, "working to rule" and refusals to handle particular categories of work' (1981: 338). On present evidence, therefore, it is highly likely that, in conjunction with the continued outcrop of familiar types of official, unofficial and unconstitutional stoppages, a range of quite sophisticated forms of industrial conflict and trade union and worker pressure will manifest themselves in the coming decade.

Nevertheless, such a development is in no way the consequence of ineluctable economic, political and social forces nor the necessary sequence of events beyond human control. Indeed, it is worth emphasising that Britain's industries and services are far less strike-prone than is frequently supposed. After all, in any given year, the vast majority of firms have no stoppages of work worth officially recording and this applies particularly to substantial sections of the economy outside the select group of highly conflict-prone industries (coalmining and large manufacturing enterprises). But equally, there is no doubt that, if this can be measured satisfactorily in terms of strike activity, Britain's industrial relations did deteriorate from the late 1960s onwards and that, at least in part, the causes of this change could be traced to the fragmentation of Britain's system of collective bargaining, to high levels of inflation, to a growing consciousness of conflicts of interests in industry, to the process of comparison between different groups of workers being heightened by a 'strike-conscious culture' and to general changes of values in the wider society. To be sure, there are broader social issues involved of the type that prompted the following comments by Bell (1972: 263) in his projections for the future up to the year 2000:

> The only prediction about the future that one can make with certainty is that public authorities will face more problems than they have at any previous time in history. This arises from some simple facts: Social issues are more and more intricately related to one another because the impact of any major change is felt quickly throughout the national and even international system. Individuals and groups, more conscious of their problems as problems, demand actions instead of quietly accepting their fate. Because more and more decisions will be made in the political arena than in the market, there will be more open community conflict. The political arena is an open cockpit where decision points are more visible than they are in the impersonal market; different groups will clash more directly as they contend for advantage or seek to resist change in society.

However, the signal weaknesses of Britain's system of industrial relations have largely stemmed from an excessive reliance on collective bargaining and from the inability of successive governments to forge a genuine national consensus based on social justice and the full partnership of the workforce in economic and political institutions.

Hence our general conclusion must be that if British industrial relations do become increasingly bitter and that if, through the 1980s, we 'lurch through bouts of voluntarism to bouts of panic wage control, in an economy which is likely to suffer from continuing poor growth, low productivity and high rates of inflation, with lengthy dole queues' (Taylor, 1980: 448), then there is nothing inevitable about such a state of affairs. It will rather be in considerable measure the consequence of the failure of all the main parties to industrial relations (government, employers and managers and trade unions) to have fashioned new types of work relationships based on the full-hearted consent of the workforce via the systematic sharing of gain, knowledge and power on the basis of some agreed principles of social justice. Indeed, the primary deficiency of collective bargaining has always been that the distribution of power and the willingness to pursue 'brinkmanship' tactics become decisive in the rewards which accrue to different sections of the workforce and between the workforce and employers and managerial personnel. More generally, too, this ensures that the positive forces for creativity in the wider society (as well as in work environments) become sacrificed in the continuing struggle for control which oscillates from one group to another but has no final resting place. It is at the very heart of Britain's industrial and economic problems and can only be lastingly altered by a comprehensive programme of industrial democracy based on employees and working people, with union officers and shop stewards becoming essential supports rather than the focal points of any emergent framework. But whether or not such a goal will be achieved or whether a continual worsening of Britain's industrial relations becomes the dominant theme of the next ten years will depend to a great extent on a series of strategic choices that will be taken by governments, employers and managers, trade unions and working people (and the wider population at large). After all, the future is not a series of fixed and determined events but rather consists of a variety of types of human adaptation to predictable and unpreditable changes in the environment and reflects, in substantial measure in industrial relations, the values of strategically placed decision-makers in the principal institutions and groups concerned.

Part 3

Industrial relations issues in the 1980s: an economic analysis

Jill Rubery, Roger Tarling and Frank Wilkinson

Introduction

Industrial relations as a subject area is concerned with relationships in the workplace and with how these are adjusted over time. The main focus of analysis has been on the organisation of work and the issue of control, and prime emphasis has been given to custom and practice in the workplace.

Voluntarism is attested by both capital and labour as the main driving force in the development of industrial relations. The prime importance of this principle, and the secondary importance of legislation, is demonstrated by an analysis of the history of British trade unionism. Legislation reflects the will of society to ratify many elements of custom and practice or to spread the benefits of voluntary collective bargaining. But a voluntary system can react to the pressures for change, being based on a balance of power and a willingness to compromise interests in order to preserve the system. What an analysis of the history of collective bargaining also shows is that its evolution, whether by voluntary agreement or through the statute book, has been strongly influenced (and in some respects determined) by economic and social conditions at the national level as well as conditions in the workplace.

This paper is therefore concerned not only with how the economic and social conditions of the 1980s might put pressure on custom and practice in the workplace but also with the way in which the collective bargaining framework and the trade union movement responds at the national and industry levels and with the degree and nature of political support given to legislation on employment protection, property rights in jobs and the external protection afforded by the welfare state. Emphasis is given not to the detail of particular industrial relations issues but rather to the way in which they interact and the common threads underlying the different major issues.

The macroeconomic context

Rising unemployment, a declining number of jobs in manufacturing and relatively slow growth of real incomes have attained the status of 'normal conditions' during the 1970s. The balance of payments has diminished in importance, partly because of the gains in trade in oil and partly because of the importance attached to anti-inflation policy, but remains a constraint on an expansionary policy. The government's strategy, implemented since 1979, has made conditions worse - although there is little agreement as to by how much - and there is much discussion as to whether these conditions have led to a 'leaner, fitter British industry' capable of leading an expansion which avoids the balance of payments or inflationary consequences of a fiscal and monetary expansion. Only the real optimists, who believe that the strategy has already been successful, can look to rising real incomes and falling unemployment in the next few years. The remainder have to turn to intervention policies to assist economic adjustment and growth: these are either the 'positive adjustment' policies on the supply side or policies of protection and devaluation to promote demand. Even if such policies were implemented now and were successful the most optimistic forecasts suggest prolonged recession until at least the mid 1980s.

Underlying current policies, and the broad monetarist doctrine which is encompassed, is a belief in the efficacy of the market process in achieving economic success. Markets, it is argued, fix prices to which economic agents respond by adjusting quantities. According to this view economic incentives are sufficient to induce the appropriate responses, and not only should the government not concern itself with the social consequences of its policies, it would be a distortion to those incentives to support those who are exposed to unemployment, low pay and bankruptcy. An efficient allocation of resources is achieved when individuals are paid their worth and labour and capital are fully employed on the latest equipment. This philosophy denies any role to collective bargaining in the private sector and demands that as much as is possible of the functional aspects of public expenditure should be 'privatised' and exposed to market forces.

This approach to economic policy not only discards the Keynesian notions of effective demand and management by fine tuning but is also a complete rejection of consensus politics, which are seen to be to blame for many of the economic ills of the 1970s. The 1980s thus begin at a low point in the value attached to industrial relations machinery and to the welfare state so that continued policies under the Thatcher experiment represent an increasing threat to any industrial relations machinery. The emergent consensus politics of the Social Democratic Party retains faith in the efficacy of economic incentives but would subscribe to 'positive adjustment' policies on the supply side to speed up the process of market adjustment whilst at the same time providing a subsistence level to the welfare state. That philosophy only acknowledges collective bargaining and employment legislation as a means to facilitate change and mitigate the social consequences of the economic policies.

Without policies operating on the demand side, both strategies rely on economic incentives to achieve the efficiency which guarantees market success. The structural imbalance of trade, with slowly growing exports, declining international competitiveness and increasing import penetration, needs to be reversed as part of the process of recovery, and avoiding a balance of payments constraint will be made more difficult as the UK oil production begins to decline in the latter half of the 1980s. In their own terms, these policies are unlikely to generate a rapid increase in jobs although there could be some growth of real incomes. Policies on the demand side, either by boosting exports or reducing imports, are intended to act directly on the balance of payments constraint but also have to face the problem of a rising deficit on energy.

Throughout the 1980s, industrial economies are faced with the prospect of absorbing rapid technical progress. Whether this process has to take place before growth takes place or whether it will be demand-induced as part of the resurgence of demand, the problem of creating enough jobs will be made more difficult, even if real national income is growing faster. Slow growth of jobs will increase the tension in the workplace as firms seek to innovate and the rapid technical change will add to the current recessionary effect of considerable market instability facing firms in different industries.

The difference between the strategies of the new supply side economics and more Keynesian strategies based on the expansion of effective demand is the timing of adjustment and improvements in efficiency. The former requires that changes be made as a prerequisite for growth whereas the latter regards the process of change as demand-induced. The implications of this difference are twofold: first, supply side strategies require sacrifices to be made in the form of unemployment, low pay and bankruptcies in conditions of deep recession; and second, consensus at all levels (whether political, social or economic) must be limited by the primacy of economic incentives. The alternative strategy takes a quite different approach. The process of negotiation which takes place at the workplace, for the industry or for the economy as a whole is a fundamental part of the process of economic change and reflects the conflict between the different motives of economic agents. Economic incentives alone induce responses by capital and labour which are conditioned by the economic, social and institutional environment and which may require a compromise solution. In one sense, emphasising economic incentives is an interference in this normal process of compromise.

Growth of real national income provides the opportunity to effect compromise. But it is not a simple compromise over the distribution of income between capital and labour. Management's target may be accepted to be improvement or maintenance of competitiveness (as measured by labour costs per unit of output) and labour may be seeking to maintain or improve living standards but the considerable heterogeneity in product markets and labour markets provides for a wide range of outcomes. There is ample evidence of some firms existing and being successful at the expense of other firms and of some groups of labour enjoying high levels of pay and protected employment while others face low pay and vulnerable employment conditions. The notion of segmented markets, in its simplest forms with primary and secondary components, is an important part of the story as to why economic incentives do not always work in the way theory supposes and why the macroeconomic prospects for the 1980s, while prima facie looking very similar to those in the late 1970s, may reveal major divisions between groups within capital and labour.

The burden of adjustment in the 1980s

The achievement of improved competitiveness in the 1980s is generally felt to require that wages adjust to their competitive level and that employment levels should move flexibly in line with changes in the level of activity. Economists have traditionally regarded labour as a variable factor of production and would expect unit labour costs to be independent of the level of output. The observation that, when adjusted for trend productivity, unit labour costs move countercyclically has led many economists to conclude that firms hoard labour and that wages are relatively inflexible. From the employer's standpoint, labour costs would only be completely variable if the input of labour effort to the firm was directly linked to the level of output and if payment for that effort was indexed to the price of the firm's product. However, there are technical, organisational, institutional and legal reasons why at least a part of the cost of labour to individual firms is fixed irrespective of output.

Labour is in part a complement to capital. In terms of plant and equipment, a fixed minimum level of labour may be required to operate a large blast furnace, for example, or even a single machine. The degree to which labour can then be varied with output depends on the degree to which capital can be varied, which in turn depends on the vintage of the machine and the minimum degree of utilisation (for example, it is prohibitively expensive if not technically infeasible to operate certain continuous process equipment below certain levels). Such fixity of labour is not confined only to direct labour but includes management and other staff whose numbers depend on the size of establishment and the operation of the business, rather than its daily level of activity. Other non-direct production labour, including catering and cleaning employees, secretarial staff, maintenance workers (fitters, electricians etc.) and ancilliary workers (warehousing, transport and despatch), are all employed in jobs where the volume of work is not wholly related to volume of production or sales. Hiring and training costs, where firms train for specific skills or where there is considerable technical and organisational learning by doing, provide reasons why firms might seek to retain labour even though the level of production declines.

These factors, which lead labour to be treated as a quasi-fixed factor of production, provide reasons why the physical volume of labour cannot be directly related to the level of production. Firms also face costs associated with employing labour which are independent of its productive activity. These include social security contributions (both state and private), insurance, maintenance of health and safety standards, statutory rights to minimum periods of notice of dismissal and redundancy and other forms of severance pay.

The institutional constraints on the flexibility of unit labour costs are usually associated with collective bargaining. Agreements set minimum conditions, such as minimum time or piece rates, guaranteed working weeks and guaranteed weekly earnings, and impose such terms as agreed manning levels, demarcation between skills, holidays, the normal working week and guaranteed payments for non-productive time.

Fixed costs of labour provide lower limits to a firm's ability to lower labour costs and hence mean that there is some level of activity below which the business is not viable. Firms can only survive if some or all of the constraints can be released. However firms with a higher level of activity may be faced with similar difficulties, for example when faced by new competition, when it is necessary to reduce unit labour costs. Closure of part or all of the business is seen as the consequence of a failure to adjust. Notice that the argument applies not only to small business but also to large firms, especially where the amount of fixed capital is high. At the level of the firm, the argument is that lower average pay, either by lower rates or lower guarantees, or more exposure of the workforce to periods of unpaid inactivity is required. Because of declining markets due to slow growth of real incomes or increased competition due to technical progress or foreign competition, more firms will be exposed to the need to lower unit labour costs to assure their survival.

Collective bargaining is concerned with the distribution of income in the firm and in the economy as a whole, but it also embodies the conflicting attitudes of employers and their workers towards employment. Within the constraints of the need to maintain an efficient use of labour, which, for the reasons given above, may necessitate a certain fixity of labour costs, an important concern of employers will be to maintain flexibility of labour costs with respect to both output and product prices. By contrast, the aims of trade unions will include securing and maintaining job security, property rights to skills, the operation of particular types of machines and the use of specific materials, and income security in terms of the cost of living. Collective agreements will necessarily be a compromise between those objectives of employers and those of the employed.

In general terms the more effective the organisation of labour the greater will be the fixity of labour costs. However it is unlikely that trade unions will be able to establish terms and conditions of employment completely independently of product market circumstances and more general economic conditions. The nature of products, the technology available and the fragmentation of tasks in the organisation of work are all important in determining the ways in which employers might seek to achieve flexible labour costs, and employees may seek to limit such flexibility through maintaining custom and practice in the workplace, influencing the level at which bargaining takes place and establishing differences in the supply of labour available. These factors are expected to play a major role in determining the level and nature of conflict between employers and employees in the 1980s and are discussed in more detail in the next section. In this section we are more concerned with how the degree of fixity of labour costs contributes to the allocation of the costs of adjusting competitiveness. We turn now to the impact of the institutional determination of wages and conditions of employment on restricting the flexibility of unit labour costs.

The impact of collective bargaining depends partly on the level at which negotiations take place and the effectiveness by which agreements are implemented. Traditionally in Britain in manufacturing industries and other areas minimum wages and other conditions of work have been fixed by national bargaining. The implementation of these minima, the extent to which they have been improved upon and the successful imposition by workers of working rules (demarcation, seniority, etc.) have all depended on local bargaining. This two-tier system is in sharp contrast with the collective bargaining structure of, say, the US where company bargaining is the norm.

However in Britain there has been a general movement towards company and plant bargaining and agreements with more comprehensive coverage and, in particular, a more formal establishment of working rules and pay and employment structures more closely tailored to the firm's needs. The tendency therefore has been to increasing separation between the firm's labour force and the external labour markets with a growth of internal labour markets whereby workers' advancement depends more on their position in the firms than in the external labour market.

The development of internal labour markets has been variously interpreted. Doeringer and Piore explained the structuring of markets in terms of the specific skills and continuity of employment required for modern technology. Radicals saw such developments as ways by which capital controlled labour. Other authors have emphasised the importance of labour organisation in securing control of entry to secure privileged access to employment opportunities and to form a basis for effective organisation. In this latter case the vertical divisions in the labour market from plant, company and industrial organisation serve a similar function to the more traditional horizontal craft divisions.

However the existence of internal labour markets are explained, it is generally recognised that a secondary labour market exists where wages are low and employment systems unstable. This is explained by Doeringer and Piore and the radicals in terms of quality of the labour. However, institutional explanations of labour market structuring emphasise the importance of restriction of entry on the demand side and non-competing groups on the supply side in explaining the existence of low-paid sectors. By this latter argument low pay measures the relative disadvantage in the labour market rather than relative quality.

The different explanations for the structuring of labour markets provide alternative answers to questions about the fixity of labour. Fixity of wage costs is explained by Doeringer and Piore by the use of modern technology and the higher degree and specification of associated skills. Radical explanations explain internal labour market organisation in terms of successful capitalist strategies aimed at accepting greater fixity of labour in return for increased control over labour. The trade union control explanations suggest that the cause of wage rigidities lies in collective agreements but also suggest that the existence of sections of the labour force excluded from the primary sector not by their quality but by the lack of organisation provides ways by which labour costs can be made flexible if firms can shift their labour market location towards the secondary sector or subcontract a part of its production there.

Control of wages and conditions in the secondary sector of the labour market poses special problems. In Britain the switch towards company bargaining has been accompanied by collective agreements specifying minimum earnings levels for a normal working week. Wage increases are awarded only to those workers with earnings less than minimum levels specified in the agreement. However these minima are considerably lower than average earnings and only apply in those areas which are most weakly organised. It is also to be expected that these are the areas where trade unions find it least easy to impose active forms of control and consequently where labour costs are most flexible. The pattern of low minimum wages and conditions of work and little active organisation is repeated in those areas covered by legal minimum wages in Britain but here the minima are generally significantly lower than those established by collective agreement and unions play no significant role in enhancing the minima or establishing other forms of control.

There can be little doubt that institutional factors are important in increasing the fixity of employment cost. However this effect is not universal and it is possible to rank firms and industries ranging from the most effectively organised in which labour costs are fixed almost entirely by agreement to those where there is no effective organisation and, constrained only by very low minimum rates, labour costs are unilaterally determined by management.

Unemployment and low pay therefore tend to be concentrated on particular groups in the labour force in much the same way as competitive market pressure impinges more on one firm than another. Evidence on changes in jobs indicates that large enterprises have surprisingly stable workforces where variations in the level of employment are infrequent but substantial, involving major recruitment or sizeable redundancies. The number of firms in an industry varies significantly but this is accounted for by small firms: for these firms, gross job creation is high but, because of the incidence of closure and bankruptcy, net job creation is low and workforces are significantly variable over short periods of time. This accords well with the evidence on the application and coverage of collective agreements and is capable of explaining why the incidence of unemployment is highly concentrated with many individuals experiencing repeated spells of unemployment. The concentration of low pay on certain groups is also explained in the same way. Low pay is rarely found in primary sector activities and internal labour markets and, for it to increase in these sectors, it would be necessary to abandon wholesale a wide range of national and local collective agreements. But the incidence of unemployment can be spread if the rate of redundancy and closure among these firms increases.

Of crucial importance to the impact of economic conditions in the 1980s is the structure of firms in individual industries, the supply of labour to these firms and the feasible forms of work organisation. The broad conclusion of this section is that particular firms and groups of the labour force are likely to bear the brunt of recession and offer most opportunity for improving competitiveness through lowering labour costs. Shifting the balance of activity towards these firms, with more redundancy and closure among primary sector firms, will achieve lower labour costs, increase the incidence of unemployment and reduce the average level of pay. Unless employers can find ways of getting round collective agreements, this may be the only way to raise competitiveness under conditions of stagnant demand: however, if there were a significant increase in the share of unprotected employment, there would almost certainly be a weakening in collective support for agreements in the protected sector so that such a change might lead to outcomes similar to those resulting from more direct government action to limit the application and coverage of collective agreements. In the next section, we look at the social and economic conditions which permit firms to operate with low and flexible unit labour costs. We will then be in a position to analyse the conflicts between employers and their employees, what strategies by capital and labour may prove to be the most attractive in the 1980s, and to what extent these could provide the basis for expansion.

Competitiveness and flexible unit labour costs

Firms' strategies

The strategies of firms by which they can achieve flexible labour costs are governed by products and product markets, by technology, by the organisation of production, by systems and rates of pay and employment practices, and by access to different groups of labour. Some of these factors are given as regards the relations between employers and employees: for example, products with short life cycles require frequent changes in production and the nature of production in construction provides a separable and fragmented sequence of tasks where co-ordination is most important. These factors impose issues for industrial relations which have to be resolved satisfactorily for the industry to survive in a competitive world. But some firms may have the opportunity to protect their market by the exercise of some market power through, for example, the formation of cartels. Similarly, the issues may be avoided by firms having access to labour prepared to work at low rates of pay with unstable employment prospects, thus avoiding confrontation with collectively organised labour. Here we look first at how and why firms might seek to achieve flexible labour costs and then consider the strategies of labour under these conditions.

Products and product markets

The nature of products may be an important factor in determining a firm's need to reorganise production. Where products are large and indivisible, such as major civil engineering projects, firms need access to specific skills and will need to maintain control over quality of products and components to meet specified safety standards or engineering tolerances. On the other hand, the specification and design of products may vary considerably, both through time and across an industry. For example, in construction the range of activity varies from custom-built housing to civil engineering projects and includes repair and maintenance. In industries such as this, firms tend to specialise by broad product type and thus different firms may face different market conditions at any one time. By contrast, in mechanical engineering, products are often once-off but the problem faced is to take a basic design and adapt it to a new function. Thus each firm must have the ability to cope with these variations in demand.

Short product life cycles, for example in the electronics industry, occur where technical progress in product design is rapid. In conditions where finance is cheap and available (as was the case under the NASA research programmes in the US), whole firms may be unstable because of the ease of entry and ease of copying products, giving high rates of births and deaths of firms. However, the increased capital intensity and the knowledge sealed into the very large-scale integrated circuits are rapidly leading to a more concentrated and stable industry.

Where products change rapidly, there is continual opportunity for employers to renegotiate terms with the workforce, for example over piece rates. The balance of advantage in the renegotiating of wages and terms and conditions of employment will be influenced by the general level of employment. Payment-by-result payment systems went out of vogue when workers could negotiate loose rates, but as the balance of advantage tips to the employer as the employment increases payment-by-results systems may again become popular with employers (and unpopular with labour). It may however be possible to achieve operating flexibility in the face of the need to innovate by using technology (such as numerically controlled machines and computer-aided design) which facilitates a flexible use of labour by mechanical means, and by limiting the flexibility (in both pay and skills) required of the labour employed.

Technology

Firms can also compete by continuing or resurrecting the use of obsolete technology alongside more modern technology. Nevertheless, the transfer of individuals between machines of different vintage may lead to lower average productivity, and hence the benefits of such change may require flexibility in pay systems.

For an industry as a whole, the mix of firms using high and low level technology may provide a flexibility in the use of labour not possible within individual establishments. Firms employing high level technology are generally large and have well-organised labour forces covered by a number of collective agreements on pay and conditions. The existence of a secondary tier of firms requires either the availability of low cost labour (generally unorganised) in order to compete in the same product market or a complementary product market dependent on subcontract work from large firms or specialised products such as high quality ranges. Levels of skill and productivity may be as high in the low technology firms but their survival frequently depends on the ability of the employers to operate with lower rates of labour cost.

Technological change within establishments may provide the opportunity for redefining job content or for restructuring tasks to be performed. Although this may amount on occasion to deskilling work or to increasing the division of labour, much of the gain (to employers) comes from the opportunity to alter the terms and conditions of employment. A redefinition of job content may require an increase in skills to perform the task or raise the productivity of the job but the renegotiation of rates of pay and bonus may permit the employer to settle at pay levels which, although higher than previous levels, may provide lower labour costs per unit of output. Restructuring tasks can similarly lower overall unit labour costs (per unit of output) and may also regroup employees under different bonus/incentive schemes. One example of such a change is the division between the check-out function and customer service effected in retailing. The job of a retail assistant is effectively deskilled but with modern technology the check-out machines may perform many increased functions through the transfer of information, such as stock control and financial control. The job of a check-out assistant, though possibly deskilled, may actually contain much greater responsibility for the handling and transfer of information.

Information technology is an increasingly important factor in altering the structure of tasks and changing the relation between operatives and machines. Electronic transfer of information can increase the part of the production process which is routinised, for example through robotic operations, and the ability of instructed machines to produce perfect copies to precise specifications increases quality control for many operations. A consequence of this type of technology is that it tends to polarise workforces into design and technical groups, those concerned with setting up and initiating production, and those concerned with assembly, packaging and despatch. The latter jobs may be highly routinised and require low skill levels, thus allowing easy transfer of labour between tasks, and the former group mostly comprises individuals with general qualifications and training who are therefore capable of dealing with task variations and whose jobs are surrounded by an ethos which expects them to do so. The consequence of such a polarisation of tasks is a much increased flexibility of the employed labour force, once the technology has been introduced.

Information technology is also capable of relocating control and responsibility. Within an establishment, efficient collection of information provides data on quality and rates of throughput which can be used to provide a more efficient use of available labour: job times are better measured and the sequence of operations can be more easily manipulated to allow full utilisation of labour and reduce waiting time. Between establishments, information transfer can allow some relocation and centralisation of the supervisory function as well as the management function.

Organisation

Greater access to information can improve decisions on the benefits of centralising or decentralising production. The improved co-ordination of activities afforded may, for example, allow a production process which can be fragmented to be concentrated at different locations to utilise different sources of labour or to maintain the volume of work at different establishments. Allocation of work, particularly between establishments, may be an important way in which enterprises improve their use of labour. Some establishments, as some machines, may only be effectively utilised for peak production levels. If these establishments are located in areas with a captive labour force (for example, where the establishment is a major employer or requires firm-specific skills), employment levels may be varied in line with production, so that a particular establishment bears the brunt of variation in production levels for the enterprise as a whole. Such a method of organisation is becoming increasingly common among multi-national companies who site plants in low cost countries and create jobs which may be more cyclically vulnerable than jobs in indigenous firms.

Reallocation of work within establishments is not accomplished so readily. It frequently depends on establishing multi-task job definitions so that individuals can easily be transferred between tasks and needs to be supported by a suitable payment system. Multi-task jobs do not however have to be filled by experienced, highly skilled, older employees. An internal training scheme based on job rotation is capable of providing the necessary workforce, although there then needs to be some effective constraint on the turnover of the labour force.

At the opposite end of the scale, highly fragmented production processes where the tasks are easily defined and quite separate can be divided between establishments and/or groups of workers. Construction is probably the best example where the tasks are well-defined but necessary only for a part of the production activity (e.g. bricklaying) and the whole activity is at a fixed site for a relatively long period of time. It is then far easier to subcontract various parts of the production activity to gangs who are employed on a number of different sites by a number of different contractors over a period of time. The system of subcontract labour therefore shifts the costs of inactivity from the contractor to the employee but, to be effective, it is necessary that subcontract labour be readily available either because the whole industry is organised in this way or because there is a captive labour force available. Many other forms of subcontracting are to be found in the early stages of production, for example design shops or manufacturing components, or at the end of the process, usually in assembly or packaging. The early stages are generally subcontracted to other firms whilst the latter stages are more likely to be put out to particular labour groups, such as immigrants or married women, who may be organised into gangs or subcontract individually.

There are however limitations to subcontracting other than the availability of suitable firms or groups of individuals. Components may need to be produced to detailed specification or high precision in which case quality control may force in-house manufacture. Assembly work depends on the ability to separate the task, especially given the spread of automated methods, on the suitability of the task to a piece rate system of pay, and on the cost of transporting parts and finished products. Much of the assembly work subcontracted will be to homeworkers but a number of industries, for example cutlery, provide examples of inwork by groups on piece rate and of outwork organised at independent establishments ('the little masters') where individuals do not have contracts of employment but are provided with a place to work (usually for locating the employee's own machine) and a gang leader who subcontracts for the work. The piece rate system of pay is however a fundamental component of this organisation of production since it relates costs to activity levels and forces the employee to suffer the consequences of inactivity.

Pay

Pay, in the sense of average weekly earnings, has three major components: the basic rate (time rate or piece rate); the make-up of pay (hours paid, premia and bonuses); and the basis of negotiation for change. In the eyes of employers, the issue is one of how to keep pay in line with price: that is, whether he can fix his price or has to take prices determined in a market; the unit price of labour (cost per unit of output) has to be related to product prices of goods or services produced. Note therefore that an employer is primarily concerned with the average pay across his whole labour force relative to their average productivity, so that whilst he may be forced to negotiate with subsets of his labour force at different times he has the possibility of changing averages (either of pay or productivity) by altering the composition of his workforce or the technology employed. On the other hand, employees are not directly concerned with the relationship between their earnings and the price of products which they produce: they are more concerned with the movement of their pay relative to the price of the bundle of goods and services which they work to consume. In so far as the two sets of prices move differentially, the aims of each party to negotiations will not necessarily be compatible.

Traditional forms of wage determination which permit wage flexibility include the individual bargain (paying each employee according to his merit or paying him as little as possible), paying by the piece (directly relating earnings to output) without any guaranteed earnings, or subcontracting. Piece rate systems are not appropriate for many forms of production, particularly where the process cannot be fragmented into well-defined tasks or the contribution to output or cost valued, and hence time-rated work has always existed in certain industries for specific jobs: one important aspect of the choice of time- or piece-rated work is the disincentive effect of each method, either on the throughput of time rated work or on the quality of piece-rated work.

The emergence of collective bargaining brought with it limitations on the possibility of striking individual bargains, guaranteed weekly earnings and a more specific relationship between time-rated work and movements in retail prices. The resulting structure of guarantees and minimum rates did not mean that earnings moved with retail prices, only that there was more force for them to do so. Employers have retained an element of wage determination, constrained by the movement of retail prices, which continued to allow some flexibility in pay levels. Common enough in the late nineteenth century was the practice of relating wages to product price by sliding scales: however, the variability of rates of pay, whether fixed through time or piece rates, which resulted from product price changes of highly competitive products (such as coal and steel) relative to the price of food, had been a major factor in bringing about a system of collective bargaining and minimum rates to restrict the full impact of the sliding scales. More recent forms, including different payment-by-results schemes and bonuses, were framed as incentive schemes but, over a range of pay, had the effect of introducing fluctuations into earnings in line with prices and shifting some of the cost of low levels of activity on to the employees. Productivity bargaining is very similar and, as is the case with other systems, is more attractive to employees when activity is booming and more attractive to employers in recession periods.

The conflict between employer and employee interests in the wage determination process is therefore crucial to understanding the role of pay in the flexible use of labour. In periods of boom, the employer may be willing to compromise, allowing labour a larger share of his additional profits, which meets employees' minimum claims, but in recession his survival may depend on his ability to achieve a cut in the average level of pay relative to product prices or productivity. However, in recession, a position of compromise for labour is less easy to establish since employees would frequently be asked to take a cut in real pay relative to recent levels rather than reduce their share of additional real income.

In large firms and/or well organised industries, the content of collective agreements and legislation has only a limited impact in reducing the available flexibility in pay levels: of much more importance is the workplace organisation, and its custom and practice, as an opposition to employers. There are agreed procedures for dispute, conciliation and arbitration and the machinery and resources for strike action or lockouts which limit the range of options open to an employer to achieve flexibility but also which provide him with a means of effecting a compromise. In smaller firms, the content of collective agreements and legislation, setting minimum rates and conditions, impinge more directly on the feasible range of pay but the absence of disputes procedures and less likelihood of strikes allow the employer to use a wider range of methods of achieving flexibility in average pay.

Employment practices

One course of action is to minimise the coverage of collective agreements by employing labour not covered by agreements. This, together with seeking a structure of employment which minimises average levels of pay, very much depends on the availability of an appropriate source of labour. Because of the restrictions and costs of hiring and firing labour, such strategies by employers are likely to be longer-term, not for example to be used only to meet cyclically low demand.

Recruitment of operatives for most jobs in small firms is possible and costs may be quite low, advertising taking place mainly by word of mouth in the local community. Firing labour may also be relatively cheap but is more damaging to the image of the firm as an employer in the workplace and in a small community. In large organised firms, however, recruitment is more limited in that only a restricted range of jobs are agreed to be filled from outside: firing is also more difficult to achieve selectively since there are agreements on the shop-floor as to the incidence of redundancy (for example, last in first out rules). Taken together with the additional costs and resistance imposed by organised labour, the level of employment tends to be less variable.

Training is however a source of potential flexibility in the use of labour in all firms. In combination with agreements (official or unofficial) over promotion, specific training can be used either to limit the internal mobility of employees, thus dividing the workforce into separate groups, or through job rotation and experience to increase their internal mobility.

Productive labour input is in principle variable since the number of hours worked by each employee is variable. However the existence of guaranteed weeks, guaranteed weekly earnings and payment for waiting times, together with other overhead costs such as social security contributions by employers, means that each employee has a minimum cost per week irrespective of hours worked. Whilst it may be possible to find employees for whom these costs are avoidable, they may not be regarded as suitable or acceptable for employment. Then employers may have recourse to flexibility in hours worked among the labour force subject to the minimum cost constraint. Thus, it is common to find short-time working (defined here as working less than the normal working week), overtime as an alternative to increased employment levels despite the premium rates, employment of part-time labour and extensive use of shifts, again despite premium rates of pay.

Short-time working is not a long-term option: it raises the average unit labour cost and does nothing to reduce the costs of firing the labour. Overtime, however, is a longer-term option. The increase in unit labour cost, due to overtime premiums, can be offset against the current overhead costs of an additional employee and is paid to an experienced employee, thus avoiding the costs of training new recruits. Furthermore, it is an element of flexibility in the working day which allows delivery dates to be met and daily work schedules to be kept, especially where the output of one group feeds directly into the workload of another group, hence avoiding waiting time during the normal working day. For similar reasons, it is useful for maintenance and repair of machinery and for tooling machines and setting up production runs. Part-time working is attractive because it normally involves unorganised labour and, being outside the scope of some collective agreements, is paid at lower hourly rates. It allows some divisibility of labour input (for example, where the workload varies throughout the week or to add a short (twilight) shift) and is particularly useful for some ancilliary activities such as canteen work or cleaning. There is however a certain amount of legislation, such as over minimum pay rates or maternity leave, which may be restrictive. Finally, shift working may be technically based or cost based. Many continuous process plants operate with equipment which must remain in permanent operation: not only are the costs of halting work prohibitive but frequently the equipment is damaged. For other equipment, there is no technical need but, given acquiescence by the employed labour force (for current or traditional reasons), the machines can be effectively run at a high level of utilisation and the use of shift times can be manipulated significantly to reduce waiting times.

Availability of cheap labour
Experience suggests that labour in the long run is in more or less abundant supply. If demand for labour rises above its 'normal' level, the labour input of the core labour force can be increased by more hours worked, by taking up underutilised labour, by upgrading workers trapped in jobs below their potential by promotion rules and other institutionalised systems for rationing scarce good jobs, and by retraining. But supplies can also be generated from outside the core labour force, by immigration and internal migration from traditional sectors such as agriculture, and by an increase in labour market participation of, in particular, married women and workers acquiring second jobs. Workers brought into the labour market at the height of booms are paid very low wages indeed as they tend to replace workers upgraded from secondary jobs. However, when demand declines, this process is reversed and the newly recruited workers are either ejected from the labour force or remain to compete with workers shunted down from primary jobs.

The advantage to employers of employing cheap labour depends on the elasticity of demand for products and services produced by low-paid workers, the substitutability between processes employing low-paid for those employing high-paid workers and the acceptability in the workplace of employing low-paid workers alongside high-paid workers (for example, women with men and workers of different ethnic origins). Studies show that low-paid occupations are dispersed throughout all types of industries and services and in low-paying firms in otherwise high-paying industries.

The disadvantage of employing cheap labour, from the employers' standpoint, lies in the negative effects of low wage labour on the stability, growth and rate of technical change in industry. Unregulated low wage employment destabilises product markets, increases uncertainty and risk, slows down the rate of scrapping and consequently reduces the level of new investment and the profitability of new investment in high wage firms. The disruptive effect of competition based on wage cutting and the employment of cheap labour has been recognised by employers whose associations enforce minimum wages and conditions in an attempt to 'take wages out of competition'. Employers often prefer the institutional regulation of wages within an industry as it limits unfair competition in the product market based on low wages and 'sweated labour', and they demonstrate this preference by joining employers' associations.

Workers' responses

During the crisis of the 1970s, the West German economy concentrated the costs of recession by expelling foreign workers and by reconstructing the domestic labour force to exclude domiciled immigrants, women, the disabled, the young and the old from the primary labour market. This has been achieved by upgrading the qualifications level of the primary workers with little or no evidence of an increase in job content. It has been with the compliance if not active participation of the German trade union movement and demonstrates the socially divisive consequences of greater exposure to unemployment and low pay.

Attempts in the UK to achieve permanent reductions in real incomes of those low down the pay scale have also proved to be socially divisive, as evidenced by the dirty jobs strike of 1979. In nineteenth-century Britain, various forms of collective organisation by labour grew and foundered as economic and social conditions changed but the outcome by the 1920s was a recognition by government, management and labour that collective action by labour would seek to maintain the real value of earnings, and groups previously excluded from the bargaining process over economic resources, status and power, would gradually be included.

These objectives still hold today and provide the driving force behind the inflationary process. Collective action will aim to maintain real income levels in the primary sector and to extend these employment conditions to other jobs; this defensive action will also aim to protect primary sector jobs from the competitive threat of available supplies of cheap labour. Moreover the strategies of income protection and job protection are related through the system of social reproduction. Once the emphasis switches away from individual pay and employment to an analysis of family subsistence, increasing attention has to be paid to family structure and lifetime patterns of income and expenditure. The existence of family subsistence is important in explaining the labour market position of members of the family other than the principal wage earners. If the aim is to achieve a particular level of family income and if family members have access to family subsistence provided by the principal wage earner then the supply price of subsidiary earners might be quite independent of their individual needs or productivity. In many families, the principal wage is consumed mostly by essentials so that any margin above this wage has high priority because it is the increment which provides for some element of luxury.

The links between family subsistence and the supply price of subsidiary wage earners can also help explain the destabilisation of labour markets in crisis. Unemployment, short time working and downgrading of the principal wage earners puts increasing pressure on subsidiary wage earners and desperate attempts to maintain family income could increase the supply of low-paid workers and lower their supply price. However, with a declining number of jobs and real incomes, the number of jobs in the secondary sector may well decline. It then becomes important for primary sector job holders to engage in defence of their own jobs, both to retain a source of earned income accruing to the family and to stave off the competition for jobs directly from workers with lower supply prices applying for primary sector jobs or indirectly as demand switches away from primary firms to secondary sector firms offering secondary jobs.

The relationship between the supply price of labour and family subsistence is not confined to sources of earned income - it also applies to social welfare payments. Where social welfare payments are set at low levels then it will be necessary to top them up with earned income. Statutory rules designed to prohibit or limit the receipt of social welfare payments to the economically active will exacerbate the problem. Limits on earnings of social security recipients encourage the growth of 'black' employment where wages are low, abuses of the law difficult to regulate and where the possibility of exploitation of labour is enhanced. This may pose problems even in booms, but then incomes are high and rising and the underlying poverty which lies at the heart of exploitation is being reduced. On the other hand, in recession when unemployment is high, poverty increasing and social welfare threatened by government expenditure cuts and the growing tax burden as the fiscal base of the economy contracts, the black economy becomes an important alternative source of income. In such periods the growing availability of workers prepared to work for low pay coincides with growing competitiveness among firms encouraging the restructuring of production to avoid previously established minima in wages and working conditions.

This view, that a person's position on the labour market is determined by their access to other sources of income, their expected contribution to family income and their position in the class and social hierarchy, thus provides both a basis for collective action in the workplace to defend real incomes and employment and an explanation of how labour is available at different supply prices and threatens the protection afforded by collective agreements. It stands in stark contrast to the 'free market' view of the individual in a labour market where wages find their efficiency level and those workers with wages below basic minimum living standards are the socially inadequate whose wage can be topped up by the benevolence of the more productive. It is the family structure, and the motive of family subsistence, which reveals the inadequacy of the 'free market' approach. Economic incentives which are perceived to work through individuals induce responses which depend on their family and social circumstances and furthermore form the basis for collective response in the long run. Collective action takes place through the workplace but the motives of the workplace are derived as much from outside as from within the workplace. Thus collective action may not only seek to resist cuts in real incomes (directly through rates of pay or through restructuring jobs) and employment in the workplace but will also be motivated by the problems of maintaining family incomes.

Direct threats to the income and employment security of principal wage earners are expected to induce resistance. Equally, attempts to undermine that security by renegotiating terms and conditions at local level to offset the effect of national decisions or legislation will also be resisted in the workplace. But even the weakening of collective bargaining agreements under competition from secondary firms and jobs will also eventually be resisted because, although initially new secondary jobs bolster family incomes, the ultimate effect is to lower family incomes as primary jobs disappear. Either spontaneous resistance will emerge in the secondary jobs to form collective agreements, possibly led by workers shunted down from the primary jobs who have some experience of trade unions, but most of all by principal wage earners (which of course could increasingly include female workers), or there will be moves from collective organisation in the primary sector to include excluded groups in order to raise incomes of subsidiary wage earners or to prevent competition based on low wages from the secondary sector.

Collective bargaining machinery, which had spontaneously

formed, had evolved sufficiently to find favour with the Royal Commission on Labour in 1894 and to be upheld in the principles of the Whitley Committee report at the end of the First World War. In the post-war period, and most noticeably after the emergence of high rates of inflation and high levels of unemployment since the mid-1960s, there has been increased unionisation of previously excluded groups, particularly among white-collar workers. But neither of these examples provides direct lessons for the 1980s: in the twentieth century, there has been a marked change in the composition of employment in the secondary jobs and the establishment of the welfare state and, compared to the late 1960s, worsening economic conditions pose a much greater threat to primary sector jobs.

In the next section, we turn to some of the major issues currently being discussed and analyse them in the context of the framework which we have discussed in previous sections. The important points to bear in mind are that the macroeconomic context for the 1980s suggests rising unemployment and slow growth in real incomes, that continued failure of markets to grow means an intensification of moves by management to achieve a flexible use of labour and its cost, that growth in secondary sector jobs may threaten primary sector jobs and prove to be socially divisive at least initially, that government economic strategies are liable to seek an intensification of competitive pressure on firms and that legislation (new or repealed) favourable to this and unfavourable to collective agreements will be pursued, and finally that labour's response may be divided in the workplace but is essentially unified in the long run through the need to protect family incomes.

Some major issues

The central target of the UK governments of the 1970s has been to bring the rate of inflation under control. There is an extensive theoretical debate on the causes of inflation, considerable experience of incomes policies and major differences of opinion on the justification for and type of incomes policy. We shall discuss this issue first because of the importance that will continue to be attached to it in economic policy thinking. The consequences of trying old and new forms of incomes policy, of attempts to control pay in the public sector and more generally of reducing public expenditure are liable to be significant for negotiations at workplace level and influencing the response of workers.

Social measures which governments may seek to adopt are the second issue to be considered. A number of these measures are seen by their proponents as releasing the power of economic incentives, for example reducing social security provision by lower rates of benefit and entitlement or by privatisation of services, but others are openly acknowledged as being attempts to mitigate the effects of recession and ease the process of adjustment, such as policies to alleviate youth unemployment and special employment measures (including work sharing) to spread the burden of higher unemployment. In the context of the 1980s, these will become increasingly important because of the effects they have on the mobilisation of labour's resistance to lower real incomes and higher unemployment.

Part of the argument for reinforcing economic incentives and particularly for bringing wages back into competition rests on the assertion that much legislation surrounding industrial relations impinges on managerial prerogative. This is the third issue which we will consider, giving emphasis in particular to the perceived link between wages and employment.

Finally, we shall consider bargaining for change in the workplace. This is clearly much affected by how the other issues evolve but it contains within it two important areas of negotiation which will be of increasing importance in the 1980s. The first is the acceptance, or rejection, and the conditions surrounding moves towards industrial democracy. Changes in this area will not only reflect the mood in the workplace and the willingness of parties to compromise on industrial relations but also will be important for the relations between different groups of labour. The second is the effect on voluntary collective bargaining in the workplace, and on custom and practice, of decisions taken at national and industry level. To some extent, the motives of parties negotiating at different levels will be different and the compromises effective at, for example, industry level may not be acceptable at the level of the firm or equally applicable to all firms.

Inflation and incomes policy

The view put forward in this paper on the behaviour which underlies industrial relations is essentially based on a theory of conflict over the distribution of real national income, both between capital and labour and between different groups within capital and labour. Economic policies designed to gain control of the rate of inflation are however formed around Keynesian fiscal restraint or the principles of monetarism where the aim is to reduce the rate of increase in the money supply. Both policies are designed to, and in practice cause a reduction in the level of activity in the economy. For Keynesian demand-pull theorists the decline in available real resources is the price that has to be paid for a reduction in the rate of inflation; for monetarists the decline in real resources only represents a movement back to the 'natural level' of employment and output at which the economy can operate without accelerating inflation (discounting short-term movements below this natural level as the cost of adjusting to stable inflation). Moreover, the transition to stable inflation is believed to provide the conditions for a larger supply of real resources in the future by creating an environment favourable to enterprise. For Keynesians then inflation control requires a sacrifice of real resources but for monetarists this sacrifice is only of resources that could make no long-term contribution to national income.

If there is conflict over the distribution of real incomes both policies are liable to exacerbate the inflationary problem by reducing the supply of available resources over which the struggle is taking place. Moreover, even if the policy was designed to improve long-term growth prospects through higher investment by using deflation to weaken union power and to redistribute income to profits, experience shows that an increase in the profit share is not sufficient to secure an increase in investment. Indeed the generally depressed conditions accompanying incomes policy mean that the potential increase in profitability secured by a cut in real wages is not realised with a consequent reduction in investment and thus a long-term decline in the supply of available resources.

Deflation not only leads to a reduction in wage and profit levels through forcing firms out of business and workers into unemployment but also by affecting profits and wages of firms and workers left in employment. Deflation could lead only to bankruptcy or unemployment because of the inherently weak bargaining power of firms and workers forced out of economic activity. However, it is more likely that all or the majority of firms will be working at lower levels of capacity utilisation, which squeezes profit levels by increasing overhead costs per unit of output and by reducing productivity growth and competitiveness on the international market as investment levels are cut. This squeeze in profit levels may lead firms to raise prices by a higher percentage than wage increases, thereby squeezing real wages. Workers' real living standards are also likely to be cut because of the higher tax burden in recession as the tax base shrinks and the dependent population rises. Even if the tax burden is levied on firms, part at least is likely to be passed on into prices and thus into wages. This increased tax burden can lead to persistent inflation if it is rejected by both employers and workers.

One response to this tax-burden problem has been the attempt to combine deflationary policy with a reduction in public sector expenditure. The cuts in public expenditure have also been encouraged by evidence that increases in the social wage do not necessarily reduce workers' claims for real net disposable income. Standards of living are believed to be perceived to be higher if goods and services are purchased out of real disposable income than if they are obtained free from the state and financed by higher taxes. There are two major problems with this attempt to reduce the pressure on real wages by cuts in public expenditure. First, the cuts themselves induce further deflation, raising unemployment and in practice a higher tax burden, assuming no cuts in unemployment benefit, than if the level of non-transfer public expenditure had been kept stable. Second, the impact of changes in the social wage on real wage claims is asymmetrical; if the social wage increases, workers are liable to incorporate an increase into their customary real living standards without any reduction in their expected level of purchases of market commodities, and if the tax burden increases to meet the costs of higher social wages they may well try to pass this tax burden on to employers through money wage claims to restore their real disposable incomes. However this behaviour does not necessarily imply that the social wage is not valued; only that workers are not content with their current living standards and will not necessarily offset increases in certain areas by cuts in others. But if the social wage is reduced and market substitutes have to be bought (for example private for state nurseries, or medical charges), this change will again feed into real wage claims as customary standards of living have been reduced. Similar asymmetrical effects apply when standards of living rise due to a high exchange rate.

Incomes policies in Britain have in practice been used almost entirely in conjunction with deflationary policies, and indeed have been more an adjunct of these policies to secure an increase in the profit share than a policy in their own right to establish a more satisfactory long-term system of wage determination. Nevertheless in the formulation of even the short-term and ad hoc policies that have been used in Britain, some attention has necessarily been paid to devising the kind of policy that would most likely be considered 'fair' and 'acceptable'. Most cost push theorists advocate that incomes policies should be both more comprehensive (to include profits as well as wages) and more long-term than in the past; in short that they should be used more as policies to ensure a more consensual and efficient way of determining income distribution than as ad hoc measures to restrain wages as part of a macroeconomic deflationary package. The various types of incomes policies that have already been tried show that there is no predominant view over the system of wage determination that is most likely to meet conditions of equity and efficiency. Some incomes policies have stressed equal increases for all (some flat rate, some percentage), while others have stressed the importance of allowing wages to rise in high productivity sectors, and in particular in return for higher labour productivity. The former set of policies is not likely to lead to or maintain relative equality in wage differentials between groups of workers, while the latter is likely to maintain relative shares between wages and profits at the firm level. The fact that all these different types of policies have in practice failed is some evidence that the issue of relative equality is less important than the issue of maintaining real wage levels. All periods of incomes policies have slowed down real wage growth and led to reductions in real wage levels for specific groups, whilst, if anything, reducing the spread of rates of wage increases and hence changes in wage differentials.

The focus on the search for some form of acceptable relative equality in incomes policy has directed attention away from the effects of incomes policies on real wages. If one adopts the conflict model of inflation the likelihood is that an incomes policy that reduces real wages will not only not succeed in the long term but will actually intensify the inflationary process. This occurs for two reasons: first, when the incomes policy finally breaks under pressure from wage bargainers, claims will be made in this first period of 'free collective bargaining' designed to restore cuts in real wages that have occurred over the whole period of incomes policies. Money wage claims will comprise both compensation for the increase in prices since the previous settlement, and compensation for shortfalls in customary real wage levels over previous settlement periods. Second, incomes policies, and the associated decrease in real wages, change bargaining behaviour. Previously unorganised groups enter into bargaining, other groups press for more frequent settlements as a means of restoring real income levels, and both this bunching of the number of groups settling and the concentration of real wage claims into one time period, that immediately follow the end of the incomes policy, lead to a rapid rise in money wages and consequently in prices. Moreover this higher rate of price increase may be maintained if it forms the basis for the next wage claim. Incomes policies can and have had a ratchet effect on the rate of inflation.

These serious consequences of ill-thought-out incomes policies have not been considered enough by policy makers. Most expect incomes policies to break down, but believe that at least short-term gains can be made that are not offset by subsequent events. If wages increase more slowly than prices, then eventually wage claims are likely to rise again but probably to a lower level than prior to the incomes policies provided the policies have had some effect in reducing the rate of price increase: no compensation for loss of real wages over the period of incomes policy is expected. One area where policy makers continually hope to make costless short-term gains is in the public sector where incomes policies are usually most vigorously applied. However the history of public sector pay in the UK has been a continual falling behind and a later catching up period that causes considerable strain on public expenditure budgets in individual years as well as leading to an unnecessary level of industrial disputes and disruption of public services. The main socially beneficial effect of incomes policy has probably been to encourage weaker groups particularly in the public sector, to organise to defend their living standards against the cuts imposed by incomes policies and relatively unrestrained price rises. This impact is paradoxically the opposite of the claimed effects of incomes policies which were expected to provide protection to the less well organised groups and not to force them into defensive reaction.

There is little doubt that one should regard the current strategy as including an incomes policy. The threat of unemployment, the weakening of collective bargaining and the direct effects of competitive pressure on firms have reduced the rate of settlements below the rate of inflation, more so in the exposed manufacturing sectors but also to a lesser extent in protected industries and services and in the public sector. For reasons already explained, this situation is only likely to be temporary and the expectation is that sooner or later the framework of collective bargaining (including new developments) will re-establish the relationship between wages and prices with some catching up for past losses. When this might happen is not easy to predict but the current proposals for new incomes policies (by Layard (1981) and Meade (1982) for the SDP) are unlikely to be able to prevent or contain labour's response. Once the labour movement as a whole seeks to regain previous levels of family subsistence or economic conditions become more favourable and weaken employers' resistance, these policies will be seen by the trade unions as wholly inappropriate and will receive little or no voluntary support. Attempts at statutory control or sanctions involved to safeguard managerial prerogative and purely economic incentives will exacerbate the conflict already present. In the workplace, normative incomes policies may, as in the past, act to raise some settlements where the 'freely negotiated' settlement may have been lower but will do little, again as in the past, to restrain settlements where negotiation would have settled at a higher level. For the economy as a whole, the continued exposure of unorganised groups to a rigid application of incomes policy is liable to increase resistance and organisation.

Employment and other labour market policies

Special employment measures on the labour market promoted by governments have included the Temporary Employment Subsidy (TES), Temporary Short-time Working Compensation (TSTWCS) and the Youth Opportunities Programme: there has been a large number of other smaller programmes, concerned either with training, work experience for unemployed young people and job release schemes to promote early retirement. The three main programmes have been applied to very large numbers of people and both TES and TSTWCS have given substantial subsidies to employers for continuing employment to avert redundancies.

Recent estimates of the effects of TES suggest that about one half of the jobs supported represent a net addition to the level of employment aggregated over firms affected. The remaining jobs supported either would in fact not have disappeared in the absence of TES or would have been displaced to other firms. Similar propositions could be made about TSTWCS, although it is probable that the number of jobs supported but which would not otherwise have disappeared is larger.

The essential question about these measures is the extent to which they permanently affect jobs. Apart from the multiplier effects of any net additional government expenditure on the level of effective demand, the net number of jobs would not be much affected in the long run in relation to the level of output. In the short run, firms are compensated for 'hoarding' their labour and these supported jobs are net additions relative to levels associated with a collapse in general demand or resulting from the short-term adjustment of introducing new technology or reorganising production. Without question then, the effect of job support measures is to preserve in the short run the existing structure of employment. These jobs would have been expected to disappear as the firms would have closed either in whole or in part, but given a resurgence in the general level of demand or increased competitiveness by the firm, the jobs are secured in the long run and the structure of employment, at least between firms, remains. In the absence of these measures of support, the presumption is that either demand for production (and the associated jobs) would have switched to other firms, if the firm had closed, or that the market share of other firms would have increased in line with their relatively advantageous competitiveness.

Thus the measures of job support have two important consequences where they work as theory would predict. First, they forestall the impact of short-run competitive pressure, and second, they tend to ossify the industrial structure and employment composition. They therefore serve to protect existing jobs at current employment conditions; in effect to protect primary sector employment from secondary sector competition.

If, however, the schemes either operate simply to defer the redundancies or provide a level of subsidy which firms regard as inadequate to compensate for continued operation, productive capacity is lost and higher unemployment results. Apart from the preservation of firm-specific skills, the schemes at best serve to delay the incidence of unemployment. Even if they are regarded as being highly successful in supporting jobs, so that, for example, nearly all of the slowdown in productivity growth in the late 1970s is attributable to the schemes maintaining the level of employment, the evidence of 1980 and 1981 shows that the termination of these schemes is likely to be followed by a very rapid shedding of labour to the point where employment returns to its 'normal' level in relation to output. In economic terms, long-term success could only be achieved by an expansion of demand or direct measures to improve competitiveness.

Job support measures therefore protect the existing structure of employment in the short but not the long run and may distort the impact of economic conditions by subsidising family incomes through the protection of jobs and incomes of principal wage earners possibly at the expense of jobs and incomes elsewhere.

Measures for worksharing, such as eliminating overtime, increasing the use of short-time working, shortening the working week and increasing the idle times during the working day, can only aid economic adjustment if they are allied with cuts in labour costs. Given the overhead costs of employing labour and the technical and organisational restrictions on the use of labour, firms will not be prepared to accept such measures unless average weekly earnings per employee are reduced and possibly not unless average hourly earnings are reduced to compensate for higher overhead costs per unit of output. If cuts in rates of pay are not possible, the current level of unit labour costs may only be maintained in the long run through reducing the number of firms. Direct subsidy by governments to compensate for extra labour costs if rates of pay are not reduced would not, in the absence of appropriate demand conditions, have any significant long-run effect.

In the absence of direct government subsidy, worksharing would have three important effects. First, it would serve to preserve the jobs of organised labour, albeit at lower average weekly earnings. Second, by restricting the use or increasing the cost of flexible average hours, management's ability to adjust the labour input of its existing workforce in line with output would be less and hence there may be a greater requirement to hire and fire labour on the external labour market, thus increasing conflict in the workplace. Third, if management do accede to worksharing without passing the whole burden of this on to labour through reduced weekly earnings, workplace negotiations will take place in an attempt to recoup some of the costs: for example, a shorter working week agreed at national level may be supplemented at local level by negotiations to reduce agreed times of inactivity such as tea-breaks and downtime on machines. By preserving to a large degree the organisation of labour and increasing the cut in real incomes, worksharing measures are liable to escalate conflict at the workplace through negotiations over the implementation of the measures and to increase grass roots pressure on wage bargaining at both the local and national level. The support or at least acquiescence to these measures given by the trade union leadership is also likely to lead to increased unofficial action and radical changes in that leadership.

On economic grounds, these measures of job support and worksharing are only acceptable if demand conditions are favourable. Their support from government if demand conditions are not favourable depends on either purely social motives for spreading the burden of recession or a desire to reduce the numbers registered as unemployed. Management will acquiesce only for that period for which they are compensated. Trade unions may support policies to preserve collective organisation. But, in the long run, the economic and social effects of the measures become overshadowed by the growth in conflict over the distribution of slowly growing resources.

The problem of youth unemployment, and the unemployment (and labour market status) of disadvantaged groups, is likely to remain an important issue for the 1980s. The exclusion of young people and disadvantaged groups from jobs in the labour market is only in part explained as a direct consequence of the collapse in domestic demand. A decrease in the demand for labour, particularly without any accelerated retirement, reduces the rate of recruitment more than proportionately: the effect is greater the more difficult it is to make redundancies, the less voluntary mobility there is in the labour market (thus increasing a firm's difficulty in lowering the level of employment), and the greater is the availability of already experienced workers, since in each case established employees occupy a higher share of available jobs.

Experienced workers will be more likely to be recruited by firms than young people where the differential rates of pay are sufficiently offset by the gains from avoiding formal or informal training costs, from the value of experience of particular forms of work organisation, and from their potential ability to be employed in a variety of tasks. Where the level of activity in a firm remains high or work organisation is restricted by custom and practice, experienced workers are favoured for their prior acceptance of the employment structure, in particular the access to promotional chains and work groups through limited ports of entry. When the level of activity falls below levels consistent with a highly structured organisation of work (that is, tasks with a strictly limited job content) firms may seek further flexibility in their use of labour by employing experienced workers for jobs with a multi-task definition in order to reduce the required number of employees and to reduce waiting time.

Recruitment of young people is made more difficult by the actions of organised labour and by those in employment. Access to primary jobs can be restricted by raising the required qualification level independently of job content or by making the promotional structure of a firm much more internal to individual firms so that inter-firm job mobility is reduced and the number of jobs available to young people is further reduced by the reduction in the number of voluntary departures into unemployment. These forms of reducing recruitment arise from compromises agreed between management and organised labour to lower labour costs or to protect employment. A greater internalisation of job recruitment is in the interests of management, particularly where employees are on age- or seniority-related scales since this method of filling vacant jobs goes some way towards absorbing the drift of labour costs due to increases in the average age or seniority of the workforce.

Access to jobs is not at all as supposed in theory where it is considered that everyone should have equal opportunity to be recruited to specific jobs. In practice, the applicant most likely to obtain any job is its present incumbent and thus new entrants and, to a lesser extent, applicants from the external labour market are restricted to applying for new jobs or to those jobs vacated at the bottom of promotional ladders. Primary sector jobs are not accessible to young people except at a very low level and even these will become less accessible the more successful is organised labour in protecting its jobs. Thus young people will increasingly be forced to take jobs in the secondary sector. But since many young people will be seeking primary jobs as they anticipate becoming principal wage earners, increasingly severe rationing of primary jobs available to young people will become a major source of social division, both inside and outside the labour movement. Thus there is liable to be significant conflict within the large unions which only effectively organise terms and conditions in parts of sectors but with membership in secondary firms or where their membership is drawn from different sectors subject to vastly different terms and conditions of employment.

Because of reduced access to primary jobs, this increased disaffection of the current generation of young people with organised labour will not only spill over into social unrest but will also weaken the control of organised labour. But the increase in secondary jobs, either as competition breeds new firms or breaks down organised labour, is not likely to ease the problem of youth unemployment. The need of young people to acquire access to the means to be principal wage earners means that secondary jobs are less attractive to them and their relatively high supply price makes them unattractive to employers. They are therefore less interested and less able to compete with other disadvantaged groups, such as married women and ethnic minorities, who may have lower supply prices and seek less stable or continuous employment. Youth opportunity programmes and work experience schemes are wholly inadequate in coping with the problem and indeed may add to their disaffection by revealing the conditions of the employed. The consequence of their continued exclusion from employment would be a marked generational gap in the distribution of income and inducing relativity in income received between the current and subsequent generations of young people and disadvantaged groups. There is the possibility that a generational gap in access to income, for example between fathers and sons, could begin to threaten the family structure. Alternatively, increasing attention will be paid to the distribution of wealth and ownership of the means of production.

Legislation in the labour market

One of the major motives for changing legislation in the labour market is to increase the power of economic incentives and to increase the freedom to exercise managerial prerogative. Various discussions over aspects of the Industrial Relations Bill and the Employment Protection Act are intended to achieve these ends. For example, proposals to restrict the application of a closed shop, to remove procedures for compulsory arbitration at national level, the elimination of Schedule 11 and the lobby against minimum wage legislation are all reductions in the control of organised labour in the workplace. Other measures, including the narrower definition of a trade dispute (outlawing secondary picketing and secondary action as well as political strikes and a reduction in the immunity of trade unions), are aimed more at limiting the 'monopoly power' of trade unions in employing means to achieve their targets. Some of the repeals of legislation may be acquiesced to by organised labour, for example the elimination of Schedule 11 passed more or less unremarked, but history suggests that new industrial relations legislation of this nature does not go for long unchallenged and indeed has in the past been reversed. The acquiescence or support from organised labour comes from its initially divided position, defending its jobs and incomes from competition from other groups in the labour force; hence the moves to keep women out of the labour force.

There are many issues in this area, which may or may not be regarded as political or ideological, which will arise in the 1980s, first as organised labour seeks to defend its position, and then as the labour movement as a whole seeks to restrain the forces of competition. By far the most important under consideration is the issue of minimum wage legislation: this is liable to remain an issue for some considerable time and may prove to be a 'test case' for other issues. Those who seek to free wages completely direct their campaign towards the abolition of wages councils whereas those who oppose such a policy may also be advocating wider and more generalised systems of minimum wages. The ambivalence of employers, torn between opportunities for flexible wages and the consequent demise of nationally agreed minima in voluntary agreements and the fear of low wage competition, is matched by the ambivalence of the trade union movement in maintaining a floor to wages and protecting primary jobs whilst attempting to provide conditions for the expansion of the organisation of labour and preventing a link between government and low pay through statutory legislation.

Much support for the suppression of minimum wage legislation comes from the argument that there is a trade-off between wages and employment. We have argued that labour markets are structured in a way which seriously limits workers' job opportunities independently of their acquired or potential skills. Combined with the absence of any long-run constraint on the supply of labour, employment is demand-determined and the market provides no lower limit to wages. The prices maintaining wages in the labour market are the acceptable minimum standards of living, which are protected by social conventions and worker organisation rather than the working of supply and demand. Policies designed to lower these institutional floors for wages are thus directed against the forces that protect workers' standards of living and prevent further exploitation of workers in the labour market. But arguments which break the link between wages and labour market clearing are not sufficient to establish that a reduction in wages will not increase employment.

A reduction in the pay levels of low-paid occupations dispersed through industry is unlikely to have a significant employment effect. Marginal, ancillary and feminised occupations are low-paid throughout the industrial structure primarily because of the existence of low-paid labour for such jobs as cleaning, catering, packing and typing and not because of serious cost constraints on the firms concerned. Such workers usually provide the labour force of a small minority of firms and are unlikely to be close substitutes for the main labour force. Consequently the demand for their services is price-elastic. However they are easily separable from the main labour force and firms wishing to cut costs frequently put their services out to subcontractors to break the link between the high pay of their primary labour force and the cost of ancillary services. A reduction in the pay for such jobs could increase the pressure on firms to contract them out. But the effect of this is more likely to be a general downward pressure on pay in these occupations rather than any substantial increase in employment.

The low-paying industries tend to be the traditional industries - clothing, textiles, cutlery, etc. - producing goods which in overall terms are probably not particularly price-elastic. However many of these industries throughout Europe and especially in Britain are under substantial pressure from imports and the demand for domestic goods could be sensitive to their price. Therefore a cut in wage costs could have a significant employment effect. It is also possible that a reduction in wages could benefit marginal firms because they employ obsolete technology which is labour intensive.

A lowering of the floor to earned and state-provided incomes could also foster new forms of industrial organisation. There is an increasing tendency throughout the advanced capitalist world for firms to subcontract an increasing proportion of their functions, for which the availability of cheap labour is a contributory factor. There is evidence from Italy that the growth of subcontracting led to the emergence of a small firm sector which secured its independence from large firms and developed new techniques and products. However the major effect of subcontracting has been to restructure rather than expand employment and there is no reason to believe an increase in subcontracting motivated by wage reduction would have any other effect.

Another possible expansion of employment if labour was available at lower prices is in the service sector. Traditionally domestic and personal services such as retailing, distribution and the repair of cars and domestic appliances have acted as a sponge to absorb the unemployment displaced from manufacturing and it has frequently been argued that this is being prevented in the current recession by the high price of labour. There is no doubt that if the price of labour fell sufficiently there would be a growth of such services. But whether this would be economically meaningful or just disguised unemployment is questionable. There is a limited demand for personal services and the demand for services will decline as income at all levels is reduced by recession. If workers were driven by economic necessity to offer services in the informal economy then this would merely distribute the stock of demand more thinly amongst a growing flow of suppliers. But there is a limit to this and moreover the long period of decline of the provision of personal services has drastically reduced the demand. Labour-intensive laundries and dry cleaners have been replaced by coin-in-the-slot laundrettes; changes in retailing to the super- and hypermarket model have drastically increased its capital intensity and, moreover, domestic labour has become increasingly mechanised and therefore the potential demand for servants is much reduced. Perhaps the availability of cheap labour might reverse these trends but this would be a long-term rather than short-term prospect.

Two pieces of legislation, one proposed and one already implemented, will also encourage the growth of secondary low-paid and unstable employment. The reductions in restrictions on small firms for unfair dismissal under the 1980 Employment Act provide them with greater freedom and ability to adjust their labour forces and their labour costs compared to larger firms. The proposed banning of any 'union labour only' clause in subcontracting agreements in the public sector provides the basis for successful competition by private contractors for public services based solely on low wages.

Thus whilst it cannot be denied that pay cuts (and a reduction of social security) would have a positive employment effect in the absence of any significant increase in effective demand (when employment would increase without pay cuts) the major impact would be a reshuffling of existing jobs and the spreading of existing work over more workers. But this gain needs setting against the economic and social costs of a regressive redistribution of income.

The Anti-Sweating League and other pressure groups who fought for the establishment of minimum wages in Britain around the turn of the century argued against those who opposed minimum wages on the grounds of the negative employment effects by arguing that jobs are not worth having unless their wages provide at least for the minimum compensation requirements of the worker employed for a normal working week. Otherwise the worker would need to be subsidised by either the state or his family, and this would in effect be a subsidy to the partially parasitic low-pay employer. It was further argued that if legislation enforcing the payment of wages sufficient to cover minimum consumption standards eliminates jobs, then this was a measure of the low value of the jobs to society. But where jobs were low-paid because of the disadvantaged position of the workers employed, wage protection would serve mainly to reduce exploitation.

The force of the argument that jobs should not be contemplated which cannot provide minimum consumption standards lies not only in the impact of the employment of cheap subsidised labour on the structure and stability of product markets and production. At the level of the individual firm, the same level of output can be produced with more employees at lower wages, subject to any technical and organisational restrictions imposed by technology and the product market. For the economy as a whole, the argument is by no means as clear cut. The reduction in effective demand and the impact of a shrinking tax base may very well mean that a reduction in wages leads to a fall in aggregate employment. The issue in economic terms turns not on the static effect, evidenced by the example of a single firm, but on the dynamic effect of inducing a sustainable improvement in competitiveness which generates a growth of demand and jobs. But more fundamentally the debate is central to the conflict between demands for a market clearing wage which allows full operation of economic incentives and leaves labour unprotected and demands for social justice which aspire to the maintenance of living standards and the elimination of poverty (absolute and relative).

Bargaining for change

Under this heading, we consider the major forms of voluntary collective bargaining at local and national level and discuss some of the stresses that will be put on this machinery for negotiation during the 1980s. One particular issue which arises in the discussion is industrial democracy because of the role that this might have through increased participation in decision-making, responsibility and control. It is indeed an interesting question whether management will seek to suppress conflict or facilitate compromise in conditions of growing conflict by such means and whether trade unions or the shopfloor will develop new strategies in such a context.

National level bargaining, in respect of the constitution and effectiveness of Joint Industrial Councils and the relevance of ACAS, turns on the value to either party of an ability to abstract an issue out of the workplace and to obtain binding agreements. It has been argued that national collective bargaining has to all intents and purposes become moribund: the Donovan Commission made much of the two-tier system and Brown indicated the importance of custom and practice in the workplace, with particular reference to engineering. But neither paid sufficient attention to the main role of national bargaining, which was to establish minimum terms and conditions of employment in economic conditions where rates were generally higher than these floors and where it was advantageous to both sides to negotiate at local level. However, if it is acknowledged that a considerable part of wage bargaining is about maintenance of real pay, these national agreements may once again become active. The disputes in engineering in the late 1970s indicated that generalised increases in all rates, not just minimum earnings levels, were possible through this machinery.

In the 1980s, it will be important whether this national machinery moves beyond the limited terms of reference under which it has operated since the early 1920s. When this machinery received government blessing by the Whitley Committee proposals, it was hoped that the terms of reference would include more general industrial developments. In a few instances collective organisation has actually had a wider impact than on wages - see, for example, the jute industry where market penetration and rapid technical change was absorbed and controlled. It may be that the system of family membership in the jute industry provided that unity within the employers' association necessary for collective negotiation, a feature absent, for example, in cutlery, for the jute case does indicate that unified response to an industry problem can be successful. It will therefore be important whether both employers' associations and trade unions in the 1980s are able to perceive industry-wide problems, such as market penetration by foreign competition or new products and the possibility of rapid technical change, as ultimately threats to the industry and not simply to individual firms and jobs.

One major aspect will be the role played by the secondary subsector in each industry. To the extent that this poses a threat of low wage competition and a growth of unorganised employment, both parties may agree to control it, something which they must seek to do at industry level. However, if the national machinery is dominated by the large firms or non-industry-specific trade unions, other motives may play a destructive part in undermining the machinery. For example, large employers may not view the unregulated sector as competitive but as complementary, say if it produces components or distinct products, and hence may hope that the unregulated sector will undermine the terms and conditions in the regulated sector: the fact that competitive activities may emerge in the unregulated sector is not foreseen.

At the enterprise level, the issues concern the implementation of national or industry decisions (such as generalised pay increases or shorter working weeks), the control of pay and the process of production, and the location of work, particularly its allocation between establishments. As regards the implementation of national or industry decisions, both management and labour may seek to modify those agreements. For example, agreement over a shorter working week may lead management to reduce paid breaks or to reduce customary overtime where this is possible through generalised wage increases, and labour may seek to supplement these by local productivity or bonus schemes. Productivity bargaining has been a feature of company negotiations but the stresses which it has put on internal wage structures and the implications which it can have under adverse economic conditions for the growth of take-home pay has made it an increasingly unattractive proposition to many managements. But responses of this kind at the enterprise level depend to a large extent on the prior existence of negotiating machinery at the enterprise level. One issue which might stimulate the development of such machinery is the question of the allocation of work between establishments within the same enterprise. There is little doubt that strategies of this type by management can increase the vulnerability of individual establishments and such a response by labour has been frequently seen in a number of major mergers. Labour's response does not however necessarily emerge from the establishments: if closure is threatened in areas where the enterprise is a major employer, the pressure for negotiation and action may come from the local community rather than the workforce.

Establishment vulnerability is precisely the type of issue which may give strength to shop stewards' committees. The recognition of issues across plants takes place rather slowly, and recognition by employers of this form of negotiation is not readily forthcoming. However, procedures for rationalisation or technical innovation are major issues at this level. It is of course possible that this level of negotiation may be a fall back position for labour: where it has not proved possible to control technical innovation at industry level, for example the introduction of specific forms of information technology, individual enterprises may be faced with difficult negotiations over implementation but the issues are then different since the outcomes are affected by decisions taken elsewhere in the industry.

Vulnerability to low pay (absolute and relative) and job loss, the deskilling of work and demarcation by skills will continue to be substantive issues in the workplace. The fact that labour is exposed to managerial prerogative at the establishment level opens up all forms of work organisation as an area of negotiation where the basic conflict between employer and employee motives may emerge. One major feature will be the introduction of new technology and in particular automating parts of the production process. Continued emphasis on the role of technology as a means of eliminating the employee from the process, to reduce the dependence on effort and exposure to human error as well as to gain control, will perpetuate the gap between employer and employee over the nature of improvements in productivity. In a simple sense, the conflict is the same as it was over the 'spinning jenny' and the 'self-acting mule': is the purpose to mechanise the activity or to enhance individual skills? A change in attitude would of course have some effect on the outcomes of negotiation but it is unlikely that the social climate of the 1980s will promote that degree of co-operation.

What is likely to be of more relevance in the 1980s to workplace bargaining is the attempt to alter custom and practice. Employers' demands for increased competitiveness will be faced by employees' attempts to reduce their own vulnerability: custom and practice is of course the acceptable compromise which has emerged historically. Intensified confrontation in this area will potentially lead to more unofficial or local action (and perhaps provide a platform for a legislative lobby) but the continued adverse economic conditions shift the balance of action towards the employers and increase the resistance of labour. A natural consequence of this will be a challenge to established disputes procedures.

Industrial democracy has often been proposed as an alternative to voluntary collective bargaining. Apart from its own inherent problems, such as dealing with conflicts between different groups of labour, a period of heightened conflict does not seem to be most advantageous to its success. Local participation would in principle provide greater opportunity to achieve compromises but the identification of worker directors and committee representation with the responsibility for decisions is not likely to be an acceptable way forward for labour. In a sense, labour's commitment to the new process has to be bought with initial concessions and the conditions for doing this are not favourable. A form of co-operation, which for example was a form of profit-sharing, is not likely to be successful for two reasons. First, it is tantamount to a control on bargaining over pay in conditions where profits are low; second, it emphasises economic incentives and ignores the basis of labour's claim to a share.

Co-operatives and autonomous work groups are seen as promising means of coping with workplace conflict. But the experience so far has not been good. The difficulties of raising financial resources, of planning investments, of dealing with earnings differentials and of controlling the pace of work have all contributed as major obstacles. Despite success in Spain and Italy, the UK reveals considerable political and industrial antipathy to these forms of organisation. Co-operatives, in particular, are a threat to modern capitalism which is not likely to be ignored. Autonomous work groups have been more successful but the conditions surrounding the successful ones provide them with a role sufficiently close to that of a subcontractor with market, industrial or workplace dependence on more orthodox forms of capitalism. They therefore do not provide a generalisable means of diffusing the conflict inherent in the 1980s.

A major problem for the 1980s will therefore be containing the level of conflict at each level of negotiation. The various tiers of bargaining and disputes procedures have evolved precisely because they are more suitable to pressing alternative claims. Thus the problem is not simply one of existing machinery breaking down, or of new forms emerging, but that management and labour may seek to resolve issues at different levels of negotiation and affect the consequences of agreements at one level of negotiation by actions or negotiations at another level.

Summary

A framework for the analysis of industrial relations issues does not properly exist. The subject itself stands uneasily with roots in economics, sociology and labour law but has been given little opportunity to develop as a study of the interactions and interrelationships between the more traditional topics covered by these subjects. In one sense, this attack on the status of industrial relations will be the major issue of the 1980s. The more dominant a purely economic ideology in policy thinking is, the more the institutional framework of industrial relations is seen to be an obstacle to economic efficiency or, at best, a restriction on the workings of the economy which has some justification in social justice. The primacy of economic incentives accorded by both free-market and liberal philosophies denies that the social and institutional systems should be allowed to condition the responses by management and labour to economic incentives, and policy should therefore be aimed at improving the impact of economic incentives and aiding the processes of economic adjustment on the supply side.

It has been argued in this paper that the motives of management are to achieve flexible unit labour costs, by which they can best maintain or improve their economic competitiveness. Opposed to this, labour seeks to maintain or improve the living standards not only of individuals but also of social units, including both the work group and the family. Collective behaviour and the greater social consciousness of labour are not compatible with notions of the optimal or efficient allocation of resources as abound in economic theory unless a realistic theory of society is made an integral part of economic theory. Industrial relations are therefore not simply issues in the workplace: they reflect the wider and continuing conflict, inherent in the motives of management and labour, over the distribution of real incomes in terms of the level of pay, vulnerability in employment and the access to incomes predominantly through access to employment.

History reveals industrial relations to be labour's response to its exposure to the forces of economic competition. The formal and informal relations which have evolved, both in institutions and through custom and practice, are a series of compromises made under specific economic and social conditions which reveal different degrees of recognition and acknowledgement of the motives of management and labour. Given conditions in the nineteenth century, it is not surprising that the underlying tendency has been towards the protection of labour, but there have been significant attempts to reverse labour's gains.

Previous threats to labour's position in the productive system, such as the Taff Vale judgment, the industrial relations and social security measures of the 1929-32 period and the Industrial Relations Act of the early 1970s were all eventually defeated. These reversals create the presumption that the proposals contained in the 1982 Employment Bill if implemented would also be reversed. In each case labour's losses were sustained under depressed conditions when attempts were made to reassert managerial prerogative and the principles of economic efficiency. In many respects, the economic conditions as we enter the 1980s are not dissimilar although the degree of protection accorded to labour and the social support is now very much greater. However capital's room for manoeuvre is more limited and the greater heterogeneity in the labour market, particularly of family incomes above some notional absolute poverty level, permits more compromise between different groups within the labour market.

The push for improvements in economic competitiveness as described in previous sections is likely to reveal conflict at all levels, from national down to the workplace. The initial reaction, already in evidence, is a decline in compromise at all levels. Between capital and labour, there is an increasing willingness to play off negotiations at one level against those at another and also to undermine established procedures in specific cases. Both capital and labour are divided and conflict emerges, for example, between large and small firms over market competition and between general and specific unions over access to employment. But capital must maintain continual pressure in the workplace and there is no obvious reason why any but the most far-sighted employer will find the motivation to strengthen employers' associations and engage in industry-wide negotiations with labour to defend or modify existing industrial relations in order to survive. The conflict within labour however may ultimately be resolved through the process of social reproduction, although the generational gap in access to real incomes caused by prolonged youth unemployment does pose a major threat to such reconciliation.

Thus labour's currently weak position in the workplace, especially if further threatened by an expanding secondary sector or legislative change, will provide a platform for a collective response at the community and national union level, the realisation of which will depend on the extent to which current policies prove to be socially divisive. In the absence of external improvements in economic conditions, any gain which capital has made in accruing more profits will not have been converted into new investment and the deflationary impact will be compounded by the shrinking tax base and rising claims to government transfers. Capital will have no obvious compromises to make with labour, and there is less likelihood of coping satisfactorily with the problems of economic adjustment. In this event, the subsequent stage will be heightened conflict in the workplace but on a united labour front, with the ultimate target, in the absence of a major re-emergence of consensus politics, being the distribution of wealth and the ownership of the means of production.

Policy debate will no doubt continue to emphasise labour's obstructive and disruptive role in preventing supply-side adjustments but labour's action will be founded on its unity of purpose. The strategy of management most likely to succeed is to combine and negotiate on an industry-wide basis to define new methods of compromise. Management's survival based on secondary terms and conditions of employment of labour will not ensure long-run survival because, as has been seen in Italy, the successful secondary sector does not necessarily emerge as a success in internationally competitive markets. Alternatively, failure to innovate and adopt new technology will not provide the basis for successful expansion. Management and labour may find the successful compromise at industry level, although conditions may be sufficiently adverse to prevent this. The onus then falls on government not to 'interfere' on the supply side and in the workplace but rather to find the macroeconomic strategy which facilitates industrial relations through increased real national income by policies on the demand side to aid industry-wide negotiations.

Bibliography

Allen, V.L. (1957), *Trade Union Leadership*, London, Longmans Green.
Anthony, P.D. (1977), *The Ideology of Work*, London, Tavistock.
Bain, G.S. (1970), *The Growth of White-Collar Unionism*, Oxford, Clarendon Press.
Bain, G.S. and Elsheikh, F. (1976), *Union Growth and the Business Cycle*, Oxford, Blackwell.
Bain, G.S. and Price, R. (1980), *Profiles of Union Growth*, Oxford, Blackwell.
Bain, G.S., Coates, D. and Ellis, V. (1973), *Social Stratification and Trade Unionism*, London, Heinemann.
Batstone, E., Boraston, I. and Frenkel, S. (1977), *Shop Stewards in Action*, Oxford, Blackwell.
Bell, D. (1972), 'The future as present expectation', in Toffler, A. (ed.), *The Futurists*, New York, Random House.
Bell, D. (1973), *The Coming of Post-Industrial Society*, New York, Basic Books.
Bendix, R. (1956), *Work and Authority in Industry*, Berkeley, University of California Press.
Beynon, H. (1973), *Working for Ford*, Harmondsworth, Penguin.
Beynon, H. and Blackburn, R.M. (1972), *Perceptions of Work*, Cambridge, Cambridge University Press.
Blackburn, R.M. (1967), *Union Character and Social Class*, London, Batsford.
Blackburn, R.M. and Mann, M. (1979), *The Working Class in the Labour Market*, London, Macmillan.
Blauner, R. (1964), *Alienation and Freedom*, Chicago, University of Chicago Press.
Blyton, P. and Hill, S. (1981), 'The economics of worksharing', *National Westminster Bank Quarterly Review*, November 1981, pp. 37-45.
Boraston, I., Clegg, H.A. and Rimmer, M. (1975), *Workplace and Union*, London, Heinemann.
Braverman, H. (1974), *Labor and Monopoly Capital*, New York, Monthly Review Press.
Brown, W.A. (ed.) (1981), *The Changing Contours of British Industrial Relations*, Oxford, Blackwell.
Brown, W.A., Ebsworth, R. and Terry, M. (1978), 'Factors shaping shop steward organization in Britain', *British Journal of Industrial Relations*, 16, pp. 139-59.
Census of Production (1978), *Historical Record 1907-70*, London, HMSO.
Child, J. (1981), 'Culture, contingency and capitalism in the cross-national study of organizations', in Staw, B.M. and Cummings, L.L., *Research in Organizational Behaviour*, vol. 3, Greenwich, CT, JAI Press.
Clegg, H.A. (1976), *Trade Unionism under Collective Bargaining*, Oxford, Blackwell.
Clegg, H.A. (1979), *The Changing System of Industrial Relations in Great Britain*, Oxford, Blackwell.
Club of Rome, The (1975), *Mankind at the Turning Point*, London, Hutchinson.
Cowan, N. (1980), 'Personnel management in the eighties: will we waste another decade?', *Personnel Management*, 12, pp. 22-5.

Crompton, R. (1970), 'Approaches to the study of white-collar unionism', *Sociology*, 10, pp. 407-26.
Davis, L.E. and Cherns, A.B. (eds) (1975a), *The Quality of Working Life*, Volume 1, London, Collier Macmillan.
Davis, L.E. and Cherns, A.B. (eds) (1975b), *The Quality of Working Life*, Volume 2, London, Collier Macmillan.
Department of Trade (1977), *Report of the Committee of Inquiry on Industrial Democracy* (Cmnd 6706), London, HMSO.
Doeringer, P.B. and Piore, M.J. (1971), *Internal Labor Markets and Manpower Analysis*, Lexington, Heath.
Dore, R.P. (1973), *British Factory-Japanese Factory*, London, Allen & Unwin.
Dunlop, J.T. (1958), *Industrial Relations Systems*, New York, Holt.
Edwards, P.K. and Scullion, H. (1982), *The Social Organisation of Industrial Conflict*, Oxford, Blackwell.
Evans, E.O. (1973), 'Cheap at twice the Price?', in Warner, M. (ed.), *The Sociology of the Workplace*, London, Allen & Unwin.
Feinstein, C.H. (1972), *National Income, Expenditure and Output in the United Kingdom 1855-1965*, Cambridge, Cambridge University Press.
Financial Times (1981a), 'Economists see yet more gloom', April 27, p. 1.
Financial Times (1981b), 'Tough line on trade union immunities', November 24, p. 10.
Flanders, A. (1970), *Management and Unions*, London, Faber & Faber.
Fosh, P. (1981), *The Active Trade Unionist*, Cambridge, Cambridge University Press.
Fox, A. (1974), *Beyond Contract*, London, Faber & Faber.
Gallie, D. (1978), *In Search of the New Working Class*, Cambridge, Cambridge University Press.
Gennard, J., Dunn, S. and Wright, M. (1980), 'The extent of closed shop arrangements in British industry', *Employment Gazette*, 88, pp. 16-22.
Gershuny, J.I. and Pahl, R.E. (1980), 'Britain in the decade of the three economies', *New Society*, 3 January, pp. 7-9.
Goldthorpe, J.H. (1974), 'Social inequality and social integration in modern Britain', in Wedderburn, D. (ed.), *Poverty, Inequality and Class Structure*, Cambridge, Cambridge University Press.
Goldthorpe, J.H., Lockwood, D., Bechhofer, F. and Platt, J. (1968), *The Affluent Worker: Industrial Attitudes and Behaviour*, Cambridge, Cambridge University Press.
Green Paper (1981), *Trade Union Immunities* (Cmnd 8128), London, HMSO.
Gronseth, E. (1978), 'Worksharing: a Norwegian example', in Rapoport, R. and Rapoport, R.N. (eds), *Working Couples*, London, Routledge & Kegan Paul.
Hannah, L. and Kay, J.A. (1977), *Concentration in Modern Industry*, London, Macmillan.
Hawes, W.R. and Smith, D. (1981), 'Employee involvement outside manufacturing', *Employment Gazette*, 89, pp. 265-71.
Hayek, F.A. (1944), *The Road to Serfdom*, London, Routledge & Kegan Paul.
Hinton, J. (1973), *The First Shop Stewards' Movement*, London, Allen & Unwin.
Hyman, R. (1975), *Industrial Relations*, London, Macmillan.
Industrial Democracy in Europe (IDE) International Research Group (1981), *Industrial Democracy in Europe*, Oxford, Clarendon Press.
Ingham, G.K. (1970), *Size of Industrial Organizations and Worker Behaviour*, Cambridge, Cambridge University Press.
Institute of Manpower Studies (1981), *Worksharing Potential: An Examination of Selective Firms*, London, IMS.
Jenkins, C. and Sherman, B. (1979), *The Collapse of Work*, London, Eyre Methuen.
Kendrick, J.W. (1981), 'Impacts of rapid technological change in the United States business economy and in the communications, electronic equipment and semiconductor industry groups', in Organization for Economic Co-operation and Development, *Micro-Electronics, Productivity and Employment*, Paris, OECD.

Kumar, K. (1978), *Prophecy and Progress*, Harmondsworth, Penguin.
Layard, R. (1981), *Is Incomes Policy the Answer to Unemployment?*, London, LSE Centre for Labour Economics.
Legge, K. (1978), *Power, Innovation and Problem Solving in Personnel Management*, New York, McGraw Hill.
Lewenhak, S. (1977), *Women and Trade Unionism*, London, Benn.
Lindley, R.M. (ed.) (1980), *Economic Change and Employment Policy*, London, Macmillan.
Lockwood, D. (1958), *The Blackcoated Worker*, London, Allen & Unwin.
MacBeath, I. (1979), *Votes, Virtues and Vices*, London, Associated Business Press.
McCarthy, W.E.J. (1964), *The Closed Shop in Britain*, Oxford, Blackwell.
McCarthy, W.E.J. and Parker, S.R. (1968), *Shop Stewards and Workshop Relations*, Research Paper no.10, Royal Commission on Trade Unions and Employers' Associations, London, HMSO.
McCormick, B.J. (1960), 'Managerial unionism in the coal industry', *British Journal of Sociology*, 11, pp. 356-69.
McCormick, B.J. (1979), *Industrial Relations in the Coal Industry*, London, Macmillan.
Mackie, L. and Patullo, P. (1977), *Women at Work*, London, Tavistock.
Mansfield, R., Poole, M., Blyton, P. and Frost, P. (1981), *The British Manager in Profile*, Management Survey Report no. 51, London, British Institute of Management.
Marginson, P. (1982), 'The distinctive effects of plant and company size on workplace industrial relations' (mimeo).
Martin, R. (1981), *New Technology and Industrial Relations in Fleet Street*, Oxford, Clarendon Press.
Meade, J.E. (1982), *Stagflation - Wage Fixing*, London, Allen & Unwin.
National Institute of Economic and Social Research (1981), *National Institute Economic Review*, 'The British economy in the medium term', no. 98, pp. 6-28.
National Institute of Economic and Social Research (1982), *National Institute Economic Review*, 'The home economy', no. 99, February, pp. 6-28.
Organization for Economic Co-operation and Development (1981), *Microelectronics, Productivity and Employment*, Paris, OECD.
Pahl, R.E. and Winkler, J.T. (1974), 'The coming corporatism', *New Society*, 10 October, pp. 12-16.
Pedler, M. (1973/4), 'Shop stewards as leaders', *Industrial Relations Journal*, IV, pp. 43-60.
Peel, J. (1979), *The Real Power Game*, London, McGraw Hill.
Poole, M. (1974), 'Towards a sociology of shop stewards', *Sociological Review*, 22, pp. 57-82.
Poole, M. (1980), 'Managerial strategies and industrial relations', in Poole, M. and Mansfield, R. (eds), *Managerial Roles in Industrial Relations*, Farnborough, Gower.
Poole, M. (1981), 'Perceptions of union members and the social action perspective', *Relations Industrielles*, 36, pp. 35-60.
Poole, M. and Mansfield, R. (1980), 'Future prospects: theory, research and practice', in Poole, M. and Mansfield, R. (eds), *Managerial Roles in Industrial Relations*, Farnborough, Gower.
Poole, M., Mansfield, R., Blyton, P. and Frost, P. (1981), *Managers in Focus*, Farnborough, Gower.
Prais, S.J. (1976), *The Evolution of Giant Firms in Britain*, Cambridge, Cambridge University Press.
Prandy, K. (1965), *Professional Employees*, London, Faber & Faber.
Price, R.J. and Bain, G.S. (1976), 'Union growth revisited: 1948-1974 in perspective', *British Journal of Industrial Relations*, 14, pp. 339-55.
Price, R.J. and Bain, G.S. (1983), 'Union growth in Britain: retrospect and prospect', *British Journal of Industrial Relations*, 21, pp. 46-68.
Ritzer, G. and Trice, M. (1969), *An Occupation in Conflict*, Cornell, Cornell University Press.
Scarman Report (1981), *The Brixton Disorders 10-12 April 1981*, Cmnd 8427, London, HMSO.

Schlozman, K.L. and Verba, S. (1979), *Injury to Insult*, Cambridge, Mass., Harvard University Press.
Sinfield, A. (1981), *What Unemployment Means*, Oxford, Martin Robertson.
Sisson, K.F. (1984), *The Management of Collective Bargaining*, Oxford, Blackwell.
Size Report (1979), *British Companies*, C. & D. Partners.
Smith, J.S. (1981), 'Implications of developments in microelectronics technology on women in the paid workforce', in Organization for Economic Cooperation and Development, *Microelectronics, Productivity and Employment*, Paris, OECD.
Standing Commission of Pay Comparability (1980), *General Report*, Cmnd 7995, London, HMSO.
Steer, P. and Cable, J. (1978), 'Internal organisation and profit: an empirical analysis of large UK companies', *Journal of Industrial Economics*, 27, pp. 13-20.
Taylor, R. (1980), *The Fifth Estate*, London, Pan Books.
Thomason, G.F. (1980), 'Corporate control and the professional association', in Poole, M. and Mansfield, R. (eds), *Managerial Roles in Industrial Relations*, Farnborough, Gower.
Touraine, A. (ed.) (1965), *Workers' Attitudes to Technical Change*, Paris, OECD.
Trades Union Congress, *Annual Reports*, 1965, 1970, 1975 and 1980, London, Trades Union Congress.
Turner, H.A. (1970), 'Collective bargaining and the eclipse of incomes policy', *British Journal of Industrial Relations*, 8, pp. 197-212.
Turner, H.A., Roberts, G. and Roberts, D. (1977), *Management Characteristics and Labour Conflict*, Cambridge, Cambridge University Press.
Tylor, B. (1871), *Primitive Culture*, New York, Brentano's.
Undy, R., Ellis, V., McCarthy, W.E.J. and Halmos, A.M. (1981), *Change in Trade Unions*, London, Hutchinson.
Walton, R.E. (1975), 'Criteria for quality of working life', in Davis, L.E. and Cherns, A.B., *The Quality of Working Life*, Volume 1, London, Collier Macmillan.
Watson, T.J. (1977), *The Personnel Managers*, London, Routledge & Kegan Paul.
Webb, S. and Webb, B. (1897), *Industrial Democracy*, London, Longmans Green.
Weber, M. (1968), *Economy and Society*, New York, Bedminster Press.
Williamson, P. (1981), *Early Careers of 1970 Graduates*, Research Paper no. 26, London, Department of Employment.
Wood, S. (ed.) (1982), *The Degradation of Work?*, London, Hutchinson.
Woodward, J. (1965), *Industrial Organization: Theory and Practice*, London, Oxford University Press.

Author index

Subject index

9781032201191